Action Plan For Living With An Alcoholic

A Survival Guide For Partners & Spouses

Lilly Laine

Dedication

This book is dedicated to

Eileen and Brendan
For your encouragement and drive to make this book
happen from the beyond through signs and dreams
You are gone from sight but always around

And to our two amazing kids
For your endless love, courage
and strength during the bad times
and the good times
You never cease to amaze us
Love Mam and Dad xx

Contents

Foreword
By Tracey West

Are you feeling fragile and exhausted, worn thin by the perpetual destructive behaviour of a loved one who places a higher priority on the next drink than on you? Then make a cup of tea and sit with me for a few minutes, you've come to the right place.

I've also been darkened by the sticky blackness that filled my head when I lived with an alcohol dependent. I've heard echoes in the void of my heart that should have been filled with love from the alcohol dependent. I know the shadowy, secret half-life you live when you co-exist with an alcohol dependent and I know how empty you feel when your loving attempts to get them on track are rejected, betrayed and followed up with one for the road.

Yet still you trundle on, fuelled by optimism and confidence that your next plan to get them on the wagon will work better than the last.

Despite the fact that I wasn't the one with the addiction, I had my fair share of associated problems as a result of living with somebody who did. I suffered with depression, I rarely brought anyone home, I had a rift with my brother the width of Niagara Falls and I fell to my knees on a regular basis with bulimia.

This debilitating disorder presented me with (what I perceived to be) my only form of control over what was going on around me. It was an insular, silent world of constant noise and I couldn't escape it. I grew up with an old head on young shoulders and as a consequence, friends would often pour their woes on top of mine, thinking somehow I held all the answers to their complex problems.

I'm not sure when my light-bulb moment actually arrived informing me that the only way anything was ever going to change, was if I changed it in me.

My beloved alcohol dependent was in charge of their life, their path and their decisions and despite my best efforts to effect positive change in their world, I realised I was only ever in charge of my own. It was an incredibly hard lesson to learn and took almost 35 years to sink in.

I've had the privilege of reading the book you are about to immerse yourself in and am honoured to be penning the foreword. I couldn't put it down and whilst it's been a very long time since I had to find coping mechanisms for living with the alcohol dependent that was in my life, I can close my eyes and be back there in a heartbeat.

This book would have been an amazing resource for me and I sincerely hope it takes on that role for you; if you allow the suggestions Lilly makes into your life and act upon them, I have no doubt it will. It has a beautifully simple and honest truth about it and I'm casting a wild guess that you don't have much of that around you right now.

Incidentally, the alcohol dependent in my life who sadly lost their battle with the disease, was my mother, not my husband and whilst this book has been penned for partners and spouses, the power within its healing words certainly doesn't stop there. It will help siblings, children and well meaning friends let go of the relentless guilt that flows through their veins, as they battle a rising tide of situations and fail to make everything right once more.

This book will uncover a blueprint for discovery and recovery from one of the most gripping demons of our time; alcohol.

Trust the advice, take the steps at a pace you can run with, adapt them where necessary and look forward to putting your mask on and breathing deep, cleansing, refreshing, empowering air; you'll understand precisely what I'm referring to after reading the opening chapters of this book and you'll smile.

Here's a heartfelt wish for an awful lot more smiles in your life, now let your healing begin.

Tracey West
Author and Trustee for the
National Association for Children of Alcoholics

Biography

Tracey is a very proud Trustee for NACOA (nacoa.org.uk) and applauds the work of this incredible charity and their national helpline. She's also a noisy Patron of the Women's Action Network Dorset (wandwomen.org.uk) who work closely with the amazing West Dorset Women's Refuge.

Her books include The Book of Rubbish Ideas, Poetry of Divorce: for Women, Diary of Divorce: for Women & Men, 365 Silly Jokes for Kids and Deadhead the Roses.

Subscribe to her blog at TraceyWest.co.uk

How To Use This Book

I understand that you can tell if there is an alcoholic in a home by observing the rest of the family. They are the ones trying to hold it all together while the alcoholic seems oblivious to what's really going on.

For most people who have never lived through a situation such as this there are only two possible solutions to the problem; throw the drinker out, or leave yourself. However, for a person living with an addict, the solution isn't as easy or straightforward as that. There are a million variables in addiction of any kind and sometimes suggestions to get out are not what we want at all; we would rather have suggestions for how to deal with the situation.

I can give you the fundamentals of what you need to do to liberate yourself from the destructive aspects of living with an addictive person; ultimately, it is up to you to take the necessary actions.

This book is not a bedtime read. It is a book that calls you to action so you can learn to live your life to the fullest while still living with your alcoholic loved one.

Exercises

There are ten written exercises for you to complete in this book and you will need a dedicated notepad and pen to work through them. This will be a private notebook which you should keep for future reference. No one else has to see it, so be entirely honest when completing the exercises. Don't brush over them or rush through them, every one plays an important part of the entire process.

The exercises may feel expensive emotionally, but they

are crucial to allow you time to evaluate yourself and your life. You need to know where you are now, what you want and where you are going.

The words, 'Yes, but,' are common replies from alcoholics when they are being challenged about their problem and asked to change. They think they are different from other alcoholics and no one understands what they've been through. They are not the same as everyone else, they aren't the common drunk, they're different, their circumstances are special.

Think about that as you work your way through this book and every time I ask you to change your behaviour, see how many times you respond with a, 'Yes, but,' as an excuse not to do so.

You are no different from any other partner of an alcoholic, anywhere in the world. We are all part of the same club with the same membership benefits.

There are 6 Golden Keys scattered throughout the book. These are vital, must-do actions that I found critical to getting my life not just back on track, but made considerably better. By completing each of the Golden Keys, you will uncover an easier path through the maze you find yourself in that leads to a better, more fulfilling life, whilst still loving your alcoholic partner.

Calls To Action!

The Calls to Action! are urgent undertakings I want you to effect, immediately. They may well take you out of your comfort zone but do them as soon as you possibly can, just push yourself through them.

By completing the Calls to Action! and doing the exercises I recommend, you will turn on countless light switches in that dark tunnel you are stuck in.

By taking all the little steps outlined in this book, your mind might find the defences it has built for you are too restrictive, but given time you will gradually let the barrier down and begin to heal. This will allow you to enjoy new ideas and positive growth towards a better, brighter future.

You cannot change the past but you can use your experiences to the betterment of your future. This is your life story and right now, you are holding all the controls. Taking little steps and making small changes on a daily basis will make an enormous difference to your mental health and well-being over time.

You are a unique, complex, fascinating human being with a wide range of thoughts, emotions, dreams and life experiences. Given your circumstances, you have probably experienced a full spectrum of feelings and emotions covering everything from deep sobbing, heartbreaking grief and absolute agony to exhilarating joy.

I imagine you've had more than your fair share of the former, the good news is that I'm going to show you how to flip the coin and maximise the latter, even when living with an alcoholic.

Introduction

It's ever so easy to imagine our problems are unique and to believe that nobody really understands what we're going through. If you have an alcohol dependent partner, trust me when I tell you that hundreds of thousands of people around the world know precisely how you feel right now.

Before you dive into this book please indulge me a little role play; I'm a fortune-telling psychic and you've just crossed my palm with silver, desperately seeking a better path; I wonder how much of my description reflects your life? This may be tough to read, just push through it.

Let me look into my crystal ball. I see arguing and that you're often called a nag, that you've been struggling for months, no actually it's years, to get a person you love and care for to quit drinking. You believe that everything will be all right if only you could get them to stop drinking. Ohh, those arguments are classic, aren't they? It sounds to me as though, even if you don't actually say anything, they are blaming the row on you because of your refusal to speak, but if you do say something, your manipulative loved one will twist it and distort it into a reason for them to storm away and get drunk.

Sure, why wouldn't they? It is all your fault anyway, don't you know that? You drive them to it! Well, that is what they want you to believe and sometimes you do, don't you?

You constantly question what it is you are doing to cause their bad behaviour and you try to change things so they will just stop drinking. You've walked on eggshells so to speak. Nobody would ever believe the lengths you've gone to in search of a sober solution, trying to find a way to make everything better.

I delve a little deeper and I see that you have come to be somewhat of a stranger to yourself. You feel you have hardened, you have become bitter and resentful, but hey, that's the hand life dealt you, so you must put on a brave face and get on with it. Well, that is what you tell yourself.

Oh look, there you are on the phone to friends, making excuses; you're sick, it's a virus of some sort and probably best they don't come over. Oh, I see you on the phone again, now you are saying they are sick; he has hurt his back or she can't make it into work again. You really hate those calls don't you? You know the manager knows you are making excuses for them, you feel such a fool.

You take a deep breath and ignore the tension in your head. Tension? Yes, but you've probably become so used to it that you don't notice it any more.

Let's stop for a moment to relax your forehead, let your ears drop. Yes, I know that sounds strange but they do drop when you relax your forehead. You'll probably feel your jaw become looser and your hairline move back slightly. There now, that's how your face feels when it is relaxed and I bet it's been a while since it felt like that too.

Now, back to my crystal ball, I see celebrations but you don't look forward to them any more, do you? Birthdays, Christmas, anniversaries, they're all the same and you look anxious. Why? I hear your partner saying, 'Will you relax! Don't be such a killjoy! Why do you have to put a damper on everything? It's Christmas for goodness sake!' All that and more.

When the drink is flowing there's a false sense of merriment and you are becoming more and more tense. Feel your forehead; the tension is back just thinking about it, isn't it?

You have become so controlling over another adult that it is obsessive and ridiculous. You monitor their every move, you check on them if they're out of sight, you constantly need an account of their actions and you do this through casual conversation but they know what you are up to and they'll give you all the right answers. So you have to be more cunning and think of new ways of keeping a watchful eye on them but they still manage to get drunk.

I see a black hole forming, a giant black hole at that. What is it? Oh no, it's your bank account! Money is sliding through your fingers and the bills keep coming through the letterbox. You used to be quite good at managing money but now, no matter how hard you try, you never seem to have enough to make ends meet and counting the bottles in the recycling box, I can see why.

Why does your chest tighten and head race when your loved one says, 'I'm just going out to get...' or there's a phone call saying they won't be home, or worse still, there's no call and they simply don't arrive? Maybe you feel it when you hear them in the other room trying to open the cupboard quietly, slowly unscrewing the lid of the liquor bottle, when they are supposed to be making a cup of coffee.

Your defenses are triggered and the barrier goes up. Yes, the barrier, you know the one. That invisible shield that stops them ripping out your heart and shredding it any more. It's as solid as a brick wall, it makes you appear cold and calculating, it makes you snappy and sometimes it's not the drinker that gets the resulting anger but the kids or other loved ones.

Hey, at least it's better than the way you used to be before you found the barrier, remember then? You were an emotional wreck with the way you used to beg them to stop, the way you cried yourself to sleep, those highs you felt when they promised they'd stop, they said they wouldn't inflict that hurt or pain on you again, but they did drink again, didn't they?

Remember the depths you would plummet to as the madness started all over again until you found your shield, your wonderful protective barrier? If they can't get through the barrier, they can't hurt you like that again. No one can.

Oh dear. I've found a dark spot. What's this? You secretly sometimes wish they would die so you could get on with your life, or maybe I'm reading that wrong, maybe it is sometimes you wish something serious would happen to you, so they would have to stop and take responsibility.

Let me look into your past a little more. You used to have a much bigger social circle than you do now; you've cut yourself off a bit, or should I say, quite a lot. You laughed a lot more too, you looked altogether better and you were far more self-confident. Where did that soul go?

I see a lonely front door; why does nobody call around any more? I see someone, a friend telling you exactly what they think of your loved one. They're saying you should leave them but they don't understand, this is the person you love, they would be lost without you and you would be lost without them. They're just going through a bad patch that's all, they are a good person underneath it all. You fell in love with them at one point, they can't be all that bad and anyway, you're an intelligent person, your judgement couldn't be that wrong, could it?

The person they are talking about is not the person you fell in love with. It is just a façade. It's as though alcohol

16

causes this alien to inhabit their body and masquerade as your partner. Ah, but the alien doesn't have it quite right, everything is exaggerated, the personality, the emotions, the actions; it's not the real deal. You actually hate the alien, you detest it but you love the real person so much that you simply couldn't leave them. You have tried to leave in the past, or at least threatened to. Even when the alien left and promised never to come back, it always did.

Ultimately, it seems that you love them and you try to protect them from embarrassing themselves in front of others and attempt to shield them from criticism and humiliation too. You don't care if you come across as a fool for doing it either.

Your life feels surreal now, it's like you're on a movie set and you, you're Florence Nightingale! Yet as you clean up vomit, change soaking wet sheets and strain your back carrying them into bed, you feel more of a martyr who should be given sainthood rather than a victim; what a strange thought process.

You used to laugh so easily. When was the last time you laughed until you cried? You used to be so much more vibrant; where did that go? You carried yourself better, you had more energy and drive, you felt enthusiastic about life and you had ideas, you had time to yourself, you felt healthier and you were happy. You were in control of your own destiny. Do you long to feel like that again?

Take a deep breath, your trip down memory lane is done for now.

Unfortunately, I don't have a crystal ball, I can't see your past or future but if you are reading this and can relate to any of the above, you are part of a very big club.

If you are standing somewhere public reading this introduction, take a moment to look around you. If there are more than ten people nearby, I guarantee at least one of them either knows, or is related to an alcoholic. The chances are the majority of them have someone they care about who has a drinking problem, or they know of someone suffering the consequences of living with a person who has a drinking problem.

I have lived with alcoholism in one way or another for most of my life. By creating my own self-help programme, I lifted myself from the depths of despair and became a better person. My husband worked hard and eventually found sobriety and we're now living a full and happy life together. I know how it feels to be where you are and I want to share my techniques with you.

The first step in helping your alcoholic loved one to stop drinking is to rediscover who you are and how strong and focused you can be. You're about to learn that without realising it, you are probably encouraging their addiction. You are more than likely enabling their destructive behaviour and are as much a part of the problem as they are. Harsh words I know, but true.

If you want to know how best to help your partner, this book will give you the tools to do so but I cannot promise it will stop them drinking. However, it will help you find yourself again and it will unleash a strength that lies within you as you master the necessary skills you need to encourage them to cease their vicious circle of self-destruction.

Think about the emergency instructions they give you at the start of a flight. They don't say, look after everyone around you first before you put on your own life-saving oxygen mask. They say, attend to your mask, then help those around you. Getting yourself on track will put you in the best possible position to help the one you love.

Your main responsibility now is to free yourself from resentment, bitterness and anger. To please yourself first, to keep an open mind, to make healthy lifestyle choices and to stop being concerned about what other people might think. You need to express your ideas and feelings, learn that it is OK to say, 'No' and stick to your values, making yourself the best person you can possibly be.

By doing so, you will have the strength and will power to help others.

Chapter 1

This Isn't How Life
Was Supposed To Be

You're absolutely right, this isn't how your life was meant to turn out. You may feel very alone and isolated at the moment but we're about to change that.

One of the first steps of your recovery comes with the realisation that there are millions of people living in the same dark place as you are now. There are also millions of people who have come up the other side of their experience and are now living lives better than they could ever have imagined. They are living the lives they were supposed to live. By the end of this book, you will have the tools to do the same.

I'm going to begin by sharing a small part of my story to show an example of the extreme feelings we partners experience when living with an alcohol dependent. This chapter will also explain what is going on inside your partner's head so you can understand why your loved one cannot drink normally and why they constantly let you down.

It will also give you a Golden Key so you can unlock the first door and take those all important initial steps towards a better life.

How Did I Get Here?

When I met my husband it was love at first sight. I found him a fascinating conversationalist, madly attractive and a gentleman. To top it all, he had the power to make me laugh until I cried.

Ten years after meeting my husband, I was driving away from a rehab centre having admitted him for treatment. For the first time in years, my face relaxed. I breathed deeply and I seriously said to myself, 'How the hell did I get to this?'

I couldn't understand how 'Me', the one who was always the carefree independent type that never let things faze her and didn't suffer fools easily, had spent over seven years trying to get the man she loved to stop drinking and see sense.

While I thought badgering him about his drinking or trying to predict his every action and be one step ahead of him, were the right things to do in the process, I hadn't taken any action to progress my own life.

Through thoughtless inaction and the continuation of the same negative behaviours over and over, I maintained the unpleasant lifestyle I had for many years. By taking the comfortable options, which actually were not very comfortable at all, I had stopped controlling my own life and I had become supremely focused on controlling everyone else's lives around me.

I believed by doing so that someday, everything would be perfect. It was only when I stood back and properly assessed how I was dealing with things and stopped believing it was the right way, that I stopped the relentless tides of chaos in my life.

For a short period, I went through a stage of thinking of myself as a victim. Then I finally realised that events didn't just happen to me, they were a direct result of my inaction, or my repeated actions that simply didn't work. I was in my comfort zone and it took one hell of a push for me to step out of it and say, 'No more!'

Not Caring Any More

In much the same way as your body fights infections, your mind creates coping mechanisms and barriers to protect your mental health.

There were many times when I felt strong and my husband was drinking and I thought to myself, if he just got on with it and died now, I could actually get on with my life. This was my mind's defence system kicking in big time.

Whilst living with an alcoholic, your own mental health hits all-time lows filled with repeated disappointments that leave you feeling numb.

Think about it for a moment; the human mind is strong enough to make someone crave a substance so much, they are willing to risk everything for it. Likewise, it is also able to develop an invisible barrier to emotion that prevents us from being hurt over and over again, in order to survive.

You may feel the alcoholic knows exactly what they are doing to you and you may believe that they're killing what little love is left. You may feel you don't care if there's any help for them any more and that you aren't bothered if your partner becomes well or not, or indeed if they live or die.

This is not a natural way to feel about someone you love, it is just your mind protecting you.

Alcoholism is a mental illness which affects those living with the addict also. Illnesses are nobody's fault, not yours and not your partner's.

Your negative thoughts and feelings are normal. It is possible, however, to hate the problem of alcoholism and love the person who is drinking both at the same time. This is called detaching and it is something we will explore and work on in later chapters.

I'm Not Sure If My Partner Is An Alcoholic

There is a big difference between someone having a couple of drinks as part of an adult social life and someone with an alcohol dependence.

The majority of alcoholics are not your stereotypical down and out sleeping in a doorway, clutching a bottle in a brown paper bag.

A great many are functioning alcoholics who have jobs and families. From the outside looking in, they may appear to have an ideal life.

Most families have problems that stay locked firmly behind closed doors and the majority of people in the Western world know someone with an alcohol problem. Usually the people they know carry on their day-to-day lives, living, working, socialising and maybe being the centre of attention occasionally. He is considered to be a great guy but gosh can he drink! Or maybe she's the quiet one that doesn't socialise but misses quite a lot of random work days due to illness.

A typical functioning alcoholic isn't interested in questioning their alcohol abuse or seeking to quit. However, as their partner, you frequently suffer the results of their behaviour, so it is important for you to assess whether you are just overreacting or judging them unfairly.

Write your answers the following questions in your notebook to determine if you are living with an alcoholic. If the signs of alcoholism are more advanced in your case, you probably don't need to do this.

Are You Living With An Alcoholic?

1. Have they ever admitted, drunk or sober, that they have a drink problem?

2. Have they tried to quit drinking or gone dry for periods in the past to prove to themselves that they can live without drink (perhaps seeking professional help or attending an Alcoholics Anonymous meeting) but have since convinced themselves they aren't an alcoholic and so continue drinking?

3. Have they denied drinking when it is obvious they have been?

4. Have they ever hidden what they are drinking?

5. Do they sometimes need a drink in the morning to be able to function, commonly called hair of the dog?

6. Have you caught them sneaking a drink and when challenged about this behaviour, they say they have to behave in this way because you watch them and nag them about their drinking?

7. Have they had blackouts where they can't remember events the following day; what was said, how they behaved or got home etc?

8. Do they use drink to function, to ease stress, tension, anxiety, to steady their nerves, stop panic attacks, relax, or sleep?

9. When at a party or socialising, do they down the first few drinks in rapid succession, quicker than the rest of the group?

10. Do they become verbally and/or physically abusive when drinking?

11. Do they get into fights?

12. Have they lost friends and/or injured themselves while drinking?

13. Have they lost days from work because of drinking?

14. Have you made excuses for them for not being able to attend work or functions?

15. Do you dread parties and social events because you know how they will behave?

16. Have you changed wet bed sheets, cleaned up vomit, helped them to bed or covered them where they passed out for the night when you couldn't lift or wake them?

17. Can they go out socially without having several drinks?

18. If there is a free bar, do they tend to drink excessively to make the most of the situation?

If you've answered positively to one or two of the questions, it might indicate they are just a social drinker who has gone overboard occasionally. However, if you have experienced two or three of these things regularly and within a short space of time, then you are probably living with an alcoholic.

Why Can't They
Just Drink Normally?

Dependency on alcohol doesn't happen overnight, it usually takes years of practice, often starting by drinking for effect; to alter a mood, to get rid of tension or anxiety, to forget, to give false courage or to achieve a high.

The mind is a powerful tool and when it becomes accustomed to regular alcohol, it can start playing games with its owner. The drinker will feel the need to have alcohol to complete regular daily functions like relaxing and sleeping, or simply to act normally. They will believe this can be achieved with just one drink. However, one is usually not enough. An alcohol tolerance tends to develop and more alcohol is needed to achieve the same effect.

Is Alcoholism An Illness?

It is difficult for many to accept that addiction to alcohol is an actual illness, some call it a disease. All you want is for them to stop pouring alcohol down their throat and by comparing it to other mental illnesses, such as schizophrenia, you can come to understand that what your partner has is a disease of the mind. As when dealing with any patient with a mental illness that causes delusions, there is no point in you trying to convince them that you are right and they are wrong.

With a delusional illness such as schizophrenia or addiction, the sufferer is convinced of the truth of things the way they see them, which is generally different from the way everyone else does. Someone with such an illness will always be able to answer any rational objection to their belief or theory in a way that preserves what they really believe. Even when presented with hard facts that unequivocally disprove what the addict believes, their mind finds a way to sidestep contradictions and persist with untruths. Occasionally they'll even believe that the facts in discussion are part of a conspiracy to make them look bad or crazy.

The addict can easily believe that they are harming neither themselves nor others by their addictive behaviour and that their addiction is necessary, or even useful and good for them. Furthermore, they are in control of the addiction rather than vice versa, the circumstances of their life justify the drinking and people who say they are concerned about them, are against them and not friends at all.

So yes, alcoholism is unquestionably a mental illness.

Vicious Circle

Long-term, heavy drinking causes countless problems such as loss of friends who no longer enjoy the drinker's company as they cannot enjoy just a drink or two, but consume to excess and frequently the night ends in anti-social behaviour.

It can lead to financial difficulties and a great many problems at work, all of which creates a vicious circle. The drinker now drinks because they are having problems and it becomes a crutch. The question flips from are they drinking because they have problems to do they have problems because they drink?

Whatever you feel the answer is, one thing's for sure, drinking does not solve problems, it only makes things worse in the long run. The drinker sometimes recognises they are developing a problem and generally resolves it with a plan to reduce or quit after a few drinks but more often than not can't stick to it.

In early addiction, the addict tends to live in the future. In middle and late addiction, they begin to dwell more and more in the past, which is usually soaked with regrets.

Lies

The first casualty of addiction is often the truth. At first, the addict merely denies the truth to themselves. They lie to themselves about their addiction, then begin to lie to others. Lying, evasion, deception, manipulation and other techniques for avoiding or distorting the truth are all part of the process.

Terminal Uniqueness

Your alcoholic may also suffer from terminal uniqueness, where they wouldn't find excessive drinking and the resulting behaviour acceptable from somebody else. They truly believe their circumstances are different. For example, the alcoholic might comment that if their situation was not so special, or if you had any understanding of what they were feeling, you wouldn't complain or question their behaviour. Furthermore, when their situation becomes normal, of course they won't drink.

Yes, rehab centres around the world are crammed full of such special people!

The individuals in the grip of this delusion are able to convince themselves - though not always others - that their circumstances are such that ordinary rules and norms of behaviour do not apply to them at the present time. As a result, the rules must be bent or stretched to make room for their special needs.

They believe that when their circumstances change, they will resume normal behaviour patterns. If you have heard the words, 'I'll quit tomorrow', and, 'If you had the problems I do, you'd drink too', you'll be all too aware that you're living with someone who has terminal uniqueness.

It doesn't usually take those who live with an alcoholic terribly long to conclude that they simply cannot be believed. We want to believe their promises, their pledges to reform and to give up but the destructive behaviour happens again and again. Every time the promises are broken, our hope and joy becomes further disillusioned and bitter.

If They Really Love Me
They Would Stop Drinking

Have you ever asked them, 'Why do you keep doing something that hurts me so much?'

If you have, there are a variety of answers you may have received, including a promise to try again, or to give up as soon as the time is right. You may also have received a retaliatory stack of complaints about how bad your faults are, or how their behaviour is not as bad as other people's whom you know and love.

This guarded reaction of *the best defence is a good offence* invariably leaves you feeling annoyed and paranoid about your own behaviour and actions. After all, this is the person you love and respect and they are now telling you how bad you are; it's hard not to take the sentiment on board.

The last, but by no means least reply, may have been a demand for you to back off, with a tagged or barbed comment like, 'I'm not beating you up or anything, so stop overreacting', or, 'Leave me alone, I'm not hurting anyone'.

At this stage, they have begun to think of themselves as a victim of your unreasonable demands to change and believe you are always nagging them about the problem. They have become completely blind as to how their behaviour affects other people. They see themselves as a martyr with virtuous actions, a slave to something.

You watch as your once healthy and mutually supportive relationship begins to corrode under the toxic effects of the addiction and may feel absolutely helpless.

The addict becomes obsessed about the new object of their affection; alcohol. It's in the back of their mind from the moment they wake until the time they pass out and it becomes their primary relationship to the detriment of all others.

Those of us who try to preserve a relationship with those in progressive addiction, feel second in line in the relationship, with alcohol being the frontrunner for attention; the addict does indeed love their addiction more than they love you, at this time.

I Have Tried Everything
To Get Them To Stop

Threats, videos and photos of them drunk, discussions, other people's opinions, pleas, confrontations, ultimatums and arguments; I imagine you have probably tried them all.

If you are lucky and catch it early enough, these methods can get them to stop drinking completely, or may at least have a degree of success. However, frequently by the time you have resorted to reading books of this ilk, such efforts are met with a counter attack or simply fall upon deaf ears.

Your addict's mind will make every excuse possible, no matter how irrational, to excuse their behaviour and to allow them to continue drinking. This can be incredibly hard to swallow when dealing with the loving, intelligent person you fell in love with. You must remember, your partner has a mental illness and alcohol has left their reactions and responses unbalanced and their judgement severely impaired. The good news is that this insanity stops and is reversed when the alcoholic stops drinking, although that's far easier said than done.

Alcoholics may put in effort to control their drinking and abstain for short or long periods to prove they are in control, which gives some relief to those living with them. However, they often reward themselves for their good behaviour by drinking again. Child-like pleas for acceptance of their drinking go along the lines of, 'But I've been so good', 'But it's the weekend' and, 'I did what you asked now it's my turn to do what I want to do'. These common pleas leave us feeling in the wrong and somehow put them in the right and quite often, we accept them.

Why Do You Stay With Them?

This is undoubtedly a question your friends and family have asked you a thousand times and you may have struggled to find an answer. You know why you love this person. You love the person they are without alcohol. It's alcohol that creates this other being; they are in the same body but have a different personality. Only those who have loved and lived with an alcoholic can ever truly understand why you stay and why you persist.

Unfortunately, addiction is the most misunderstood mental illness. When dealing with someone that has schizophrenia, you know you are dealing with someone who isn't in their right mind and you know also that their symptoms can be rectified or controlled with medication.

However, with alcohol addiction, the only remedy is to stop drinking alcohol and so it is seen as a voluntary choice and decision.

It is believed by those who don't understand the illness, that the drinker is not suffering from mental delusions, they are just being selfish and they should quite simply stop drinking.

The Problem Spreads

It is hard to share your problems with people who don't understand, with answers like, 'Just tell her to stop', 'He's so selfish', 'Threaten to leave them', and 'Put your foot down', being typical responses.

Invariably, they urge us to stop sharing and sometimes we are so ashamed of the problem or afraid of how people will react, we keep it as a secret and avoid too much interaction with friends or family.

We become isolated and combined with the constant emotional roller-coaster of fear, anger, confusion, depression, bitterness and false hope we find ourselves immersed in, it often leads to our own mental health being adversely affected.

Here are some of the typical symptoms partners experience that you may be able to relate to:

Hiding the truth: those living with an alcoholic can devote a great deal of time and energy to hiding the alcoholic's problems. They regularly make excuses and apologise for the behaviour of the alcoholic to employers, co-workers, friends and relatives.

Acting out: this is a psychological term for the impulsive, immature and sometimes irresponsible behaviour that a person uses in order to handle internal emotional stress.

The partner may develop an, 'If you can't beat them, join them' attitude and drink with the alcoholic for a period; this is often short-lived. Finally, hostility, bitterness and anger erupt into loud arguments and out-of-character physical attacks.

They try to alter the drinker's behaviour: most people who live with an addictive person try to get them to change and behave in a more socially acceptable fashion. They struggle with various methods for months, even years, occasionally their whole life, because they believe all will be well when their partner gives up drinking.

Unfortunately, this rarely works, no matter how hard they try. In fact, the more they attempt to change the addict, the more the addict rears up and fights the attempts. The alcoholic will often claim that all the nagging makes them drink even more.

Becoming isolated: as the alcoholic's problems increase, contact with friends, neighbours and relatives invariably decreases in order to avoid shame and embarrassment.

Giving up: depression sets in, apathy, pain and chronic fatigue often accompany it with few rare moments of authentic joy, comfort and relaxation.

If you identify with any of these symptoms, you are experiencing them alongside millions of other people around the globe. Collectively, you are all suffering the normal mental health consequences of living in a destructive, long-term, co-dependent relationship.

You can't live with them and you can't live without them!

Am I Mentally Unwell Too?

I hate to be the bearer of bad news, but quite possibly yes.

However, the good news is that you don't have to wait for your partner to stop drinking and get better, in order for you to get better.

Your world view has been severely impaired by living with your alcoholic partner and it is highly likely to have had a negative impact on your general outlook.

Don't worry, finding a solution and repairing the damage to yourself is within your control.

The fact that you're reading this book means you've taken serious steps towards changing your life and hopefully encouraging your partner to change theirs too. That took a positive, conscious decision on your part.

As you work your way through the book you might suddenly come to realise that you've been suffering with depression or anxiety, which has probably impaired your judgement. It's nothing to worry about or be ashamed of.

Make an appointment to see your doctor or counsellor as soon as possible to discuss your situation. They have a wealth of solutions that will help you find a better balance with your mental well-being and ultimately, this will allow you to move smoothly ahead with your plans.

Providing there are no risks of violence from your partner, there are several self-help steps you can take towards living a full and enjoyable life, while still living with your alcoholic loved one. Taking these steps is the most helpful thing you can do to encourage your partner to get well too.

Let's get started with the first Golden Key to unlock a new and better life.

Golden Key One

Talk To Others

In A Similar Situation

Isolation and secrecy are damaging to our health. Talking honestly and openly to people who understand what we're going through is great therapy.

In 131 countries across the globe there are 24,000 groups of people in similar, sometimes near identical situations to you. They meet up on a weekly basis to share and support each other anonymously in a non-judgemental way.

They are called Al-Anon groups and there are usually several different groups running in an area, so you should be able to find one you feel comfortable in and that suits your availability to attend, when you feel the need.

The people that go to the meetings are just like you and me, they are living with, or care about, somebody who is addicted to alcohol and they have been affected by it.

Nobody will tell you what to do or berate you for what you feel you are doing wrong. By sharing and listening to how others deal with similar situations in a healthy way, you will find your own solutions to daily problems.

The group members will not quiz you about who you are or where you are from, as the name implies, it's anonymous. The meetings are free and you do not even have to give your name. You just arrive and listen and talk if you want to. No one will question you if you stay silent.

If you don't feel you're ready for a face to face meeting, try an online meeting instead. InTheRooms.com offer support groups and online meetings, with over 287,000 members around the world who are either recovering addicts or family members of addicts.

There is also Stepchat, an online recovery chat-room service, which currently has over 100 scheduled meetings online per week at all times of the day and night, covering topics directly relating to being a partner of an alcoholic and many associated issues too.

For further details and contact information for these key groups see the resources pages.

Call to Action!

Find out where the Al-Anon groups are in your area or a nearby town. Your GP or local health centre may be able to provide you with this information, or you could do a simple search online by visiting their website. Jot down the meeting places, days and times in your notebook for future reference.

You're Obsessed With Their Drinking

Those living with alcoholism are quite used to living in chaos. You hate to see your partner change because of what they drink and you hate being lied to and being on your guard all the time.

You become obsessed with controlling their drinking and frequently forget about your own needs; they are secondary. You're convinced that getting them to quit is the most important thing in your life. Surely once that is fixed, everything else will fall into place?

If your relationship is suffering as a consequence of a person's drinking, you can be sure of the fact that you both have problems related to alcohol. Maybe this person is not a severe alcoholic but the difficulties that have arisen as a consequence of his or her abuse has also forced you into a destructive process; if drinking is causing problems, then there is indeed a drinking problem.

The road to a better life for both of you begins with the understanding that you cannot control the alcoholic's drinking behaviour long-term and that you cannot control them or what they do.

Change only comes from within and that applies to you, as much as them.

Once you understand and accept this, you'll realise that you can only take responsibility for your life and your own actions and that simple action may have a positive effect on the behaviour of your alcoholic partner.

You Want Change Now!

Al-Anon and Alcoholics Anonymous are not affiliated with any religion or sect but there is a common prayer that is said at the end of their meetings:

> *God grant me the serenity*
> *To accept the things I cannot change*
> *The courage to change the things I can*
> *And the wisdom to know the difference*

Even if you don't believe in God, think about the words. To accept the things you cannot change you need to develop serenity, but you need to be wise enough to recognise the things you can change and you need to muster up the courage to do so.

Impatience is a common trait for an alcoholic and their partners have a tendency to develop it too. We want change desperately and we want it now!

Take your recovery slowly. You are about to start growing again as a person and you need to force yourself to have patience so you can develop at your own speed.

Don't force change however. Your mind is a powerful tool and it has probably spent a significant amount of time building a perfect and intricate barrier to shield you against the advancing tide of emotional blows, so treat yourself and your mind gently.

Chapter 2

You Who?

Who Is Ruining Your Life?

Those who live with alcoholism often see themselves as martyrs or victims of alcoholic behaviour. They shoulder all the responsibility, they sacrifice their own interests and lives to keep things together and they tend to forget the fact that the alcoholic is actually a very capable adult.

The reason the alcoholic continues to drink is because they are not taking responsibility for their actions, they have a mental illness which causes them to be self-indulgent and their lives have stagnated as a result. This stagnation often begins around the time their drinking started to become a problem. This is why alcoholics often act immaturely, as they are determined to do what they want to do and to get what they want.

Think for a moment about how you are behaving. Are you taking responsibility for your life? Are you taking actions to stop your partner drinking and in so doing are you neglecting your own development? Did your life also begin to stagnate from the time when your partner's drinking became a problem?

By sacrificing your day-to-day life and attempting to control another human being's behaviour or actions, you are not doing yourself, or anyone else, any favours. You are not winning points in Heaven nor are you helping your partner. In fact if anything, you are probably inadvertently aiding them on their quest to stay drinking. This is called enabling and we'll deal with it later in the book.

I bet when you read the title of this chapter you immediately thought I was referring to your alcoholic loved one; that's incorrect, I'm talking about you!

Now, you may find this next statement rather unsettling,

so brace yourself. The person responsible for your daily life continuing to be difficult, depressing or miserable, is not your partner, your family or your God, it is you.

You are responsible for how you let people affect you and how you affect other people. You are an individual with responsibility for every action and decision you make. You are responsible for your words, your responses, your emotions and your decisions. Maybe this was not always the case, perhaps you had an arranged marriage, or maybe you were young and foolish when you got into this relationship but that was then and this is now!

Exercise 1: Actions And Decisions

For every action you do today I want you to say to yourself:

I, (your name), am responsible for making this dinner, turning on this computer, taking the children to school, etc.

Do this as well for every decision you make:

I, (your name), am responsible for deciding to make the dinner, buy the groceries, read a book, have a shower, pray, stay in bed, watch my favourite TV programme, ring my mum for a friendly chat.

Don't forget to say it before you deal with any unpleasant or yucky stuff too!

I (your name), am responsible for clearing up after my alcoholic partner, hiding their drink, buying their drink, calling their boss to say they can't make it in to work, making an excuse for why they can't be somewhere, opening and dealing with the bills, telling them they need to shower and clean themselves up, waking them up to eat dinner, changing wet bedding or cleaning up vomit, hiding evidence of their drinking from the family and so on.

In your notebook, make a list of twenty things you took responsibility for in the last week (or month if you prefer) and include ten unpleasant things of this nature.

Chapter 3

Taking Responsibility

'It's your fault that I drink. Right, that's it, I'm tired of your nagging, I'm going for a drink and who can blame me when living with you. If you had/hadn't done that, I wouldn't be drinking now'.

The majority of partners of alcoholics have had this type of blame laid at their door at some time or other. It's hard not to take it on board, as we probably were nagging or doing the thing they're blaming us for, that led to their behaviour. We often concede with a, 'Yes, it is partly my fault they act the way they do'.

Earlier, I explained that it's not the alcoholic ruining your life. You are an adult and responsible for your actions and reactions. Well, the same goes for your alcoholic loved one. They are adults too and entirely responsible for their actions and reactions.

You are not responsible for ruining their day or their life. You are both adults and individuals who fell in love and now things have got out of control. You both need to regain control of your own lives again and stop trying to control each other's. You cannot control your loved one or their behaviour but you can control your own.

I want to show you how to gain strength to identify and aspire towards a worthwhile life while still loving the person who has the alcohol addiction problem.

Call To Action!

From today, you are no longer going to blame anybody or your circumstances, for the way you feel, the way you act, the way you are, the person you are, the things you say or the actions you take. From today, you are no longer going to allow any other adult to blame you for

---

how they feel, act or live. You do not have to say this aloud but you should remind yourself daily, that every adult is responsible for their own actions.

Taking Responsibility For You

To date, you have left your fate and happiness in the hands of your partner and let it be influenced by their actions and behaviour. They are a person you love but their actions and decisions are awful!

You may feel you're suffering the consequences of bad choices, 'I should never have married him', 'I should never have had children with her' or 'I shouldn't have given them control of our bank account' and so on.

These are decisions from your past which cannot be changed, but you do have the power to change the future.

When you look back on the period of your partner's drinking, it may seem like you've had years of the same thing with the same routine of crisis management, financial disasters and an all consuming time of constantly trying to control their life and actions, whilst neglecting yourself and your life.

You see yourself as a survivor, at times a martyr for the cause, a warrior, a saint, a strong-minded person but when you get through this episode in your life and look back on it, you will probably feel like a fool for not taking real responsibility earlier and as a result, living in chaos for such a long time, years, maybe even decades.

Do not regret that time. There's absolutely no point in regretting the past. Praise yourself instead for eventually garnering enough strength to pull your feet out of the sludge and taking a hard gallop along a better path.

You will do this by taking 100% responsibility for your own life, for how it's going and the path it is taking.

Exercise 2: Achievements

Think back on all the significant things you've achieved in your life, however large or small. These could include reaching a certain standard of education, getting an award, bringing a child into the world, completing a lifelong ambition, learning how to play an instrument, assisting a charity, paying off a debt, decorating a room or decorating a cake. It might assist the process if you divide your life into sections of five or ten years, then write a list of five things for each time period.

So the first ten years might include finishing each year of school, accumulating scout badges, going to swimming classes, potty training, learning to speak and so on.

Your last five or ten might include events like learning to drive, negotiating a loan or rent for your house, teaching your child their first nursery rhyme, getting an important job and things of a similar ilk. From these, compile a list of your top ten life achievements in your notebook.

Research shows the more you acknowledge your past successes, the more confident you'll become in taking on this new challenge of rebuilding your life and successfully accomplishing what you set out to do.

Keep your list close to hand and refer back to it whenever you need to remind yourself about your ability to achieve change in your current situation.

When you are feeling low and weak, look back on this list and it will give you strength to know you can achieve great things, you can stay strong and you can do a lot when you put your mind to it.

Chapter 4

Actions And Reactions

You want your alcoholic loved one to take responsibility for their actions and stop the current behaviour that is wasting away their life, don't you? However, for you to be of assistance to them in this endeavour, you need to apply the same formula to your own life.

To stop them behaving the way they do, you need to stop behaving the way you do and stop blaming them for your resulting unhappy life. If you don't want to be a doormat, then get up off the floor!

Your life path and quality of life is neither their fault, nor a result of their actions. It is a result of your reactions. It also works the same in reverse; their drinking and quality of life or life choices, are not a result of your actions.

Call To Action!

Look at your partner's life. Think about how they are wasting precious days of their life. Now think about your own life, how many days recently have you spent looking after or nurturing your own dreams and happiness? If the answer is none, consider those days where you simply existed and dealt with the results of their addiction, as wasted too.

Make a firm decision never to waste another day and do something every day to improve your life, no matter how small or incidental it is.

100% Responsibility

To make any progress you have to take 100% responsibility for every element of your life, including your health, happiness, finances and emotions. This isn't easy but once you start reclaiming control of yourself, you will feel an immense burden lift from your shoulders.

If you're a parent, you'll be used to doing this in your children's lives, which makes summoning the strength to do it for your alcohol dependent loved one all the more difficult. However, you had the strength to pick up this book and start reading it, so you are already on the road to taking back responsibility and moving forward from the sludge of stagnation.

In order to take 100% responsibility, you must stop blaming the alcoholic for the circumstances you find yourself in and stop being the victim, stop making excuses, stop feeling sorry for yourself, stop deeming yourself a saint or martyr, stop blaming them for the decisions you make and the reasons you can't do things.

Your current life is the result of all your successes and failures. It is only by acknowledging that you've created your life to date, that you can move on and create a better life for you and your family.

You may be screaming, '100% responsibility? I already shoulder 200% responsibility and more!'

If you don't currently live your life, you have to change. Notice I didn't say you have to change your alcoholic's behaviour or life, but yours.

I realise this may sound difficult and complicated when your lives are entwined and woven together by the kids, the finances, the dog, the cat, the house, the car, the bills and the debt but these are simply excuses for you not to regain control of your life.

You are not responsible for the operations of the entire Universe but you are responsible for your own actions. You do not need to take care of everything and everybody and you do have a choice in this matter.

Yes, there are elements which are part of your life that you need to deal with and take responsibility for but if you want different results from your life you need to change the way you currently deal with things. In other words, if you keep using the same recipe, you'll keep baking the same cake.

Call To Action!

Keep a check on how you think and how you speak about the alcoholic's effect on your life. If you find yourself blaming them for your quality of life, stop yourself and say out loud, 'This is my life, it's a great life and I am in control of it, no one else can control it'.

Taking Responsibility
For The Alcoholic

It is human nature to shield, protect and nurture the ones we love. Living with an alcoholic loved one challenges this basic instinct. A lot of things go wrong in the lives of drinkers in respect of their home, work, family, appointments and so on and all tend to suffer to various degrees.

Human nature kicks in and we often help by sorting out the things that have gone wrong, doing chores like running errands for them, buying drinks to get them through a bad period, cleaning up after them, making excuses at their workplace or to friends or by cancelling their appointments.

When it comes to loving and caring for an alcoholic, we tend to help them through their day in whatever way we can in order to survive and live with hope. We adopt their responsibilities as our own and in the short term this is helpful for the drinker and they appreciate our assistance because without it, their life as an alcoholic would be so much more difficult.

Think about how you help your alcoholic partner. Now think about what that help and support is actually doing for the drinker? Does it make it easier or more difficult for them to continue drinking? Are you enabling their bad behaviour further by not letting them see what they are doing to themselves and others around them?

Think about it, if your partner's bottles, spillages and mess are all cleaned up and tidied away by the time they sober up, they have no evidence of how serious their drinking is. Their deluded mind will look around and see everything is just fine, therefore their drinking must be in control and it's OK to continue doing so.

If they don't have anyone to answer to regarding their behaviour because you have picked up the pieces, made excuses on their behalf and swum oceans to cover up for them, they don't have to deal with any awkward questions.

In other words, they don't have to face up to the consequences of their behaviour or actions, because you have already cushioned the blow or stopped oncoming problems in their tracks.

So, if the alcohol dependent doesn't have to face up to the fact that their drinking is causing problems in their life, why should they stop drinking? There's no motivation to do so when you solve their problems, therefore they can continue drinking and why not? It clearly isn't causing any harm!

What you are doing is putting off the inevitable and enabling them to continue on the road to destruction. Things are not going to improve, indeed they are likely to get worse if you continue to enable their bad behaviour. It is clearly better for them to face things that are going wrong in order to truly realise what they are doing.

Debt

When the bills are unpaid and overdue, don't take a second job to bail out an alcoholic who won't work. If you work to pay all the bills and the alcoholic is not working through choice, you may want to consider leaving for a while and forcing the responsibility on to the alcoholic.

If they lose their home, it is not your responsibility. Of course, if you are living together and they are the main breadwinner, dealing with debt can be a difficult task. This issue is unquestionably one of the most troublesome ones to cope with during this process of change. Once you have accepted your responsibility and are providing a home for yourself and any children, it is the alcoholic's responsibility to do the same for themselves.

Call To Action!

Start a secret emergency fund. Put a little money aside regularly and don't be tempted to dip into it. This is your cash reserve in case you have to get out of your situation quickly. Aim to have enough put aside for a hotel, phone calls, food and fuel to drive or the taxi fare to get away.

Golden Key Two

To Help, Stop Helping

Stop enabling your partner's behaviour but do it without fighting, threats or bribery. Simply stop doing all the things that are the alcoholic's responsibility and concentrate on you. The more you do, the more the alcoholic will have to concentrate on themselves.

Do not bail them out of trouble for drink driving, do not lie for, or to them about how much they drink. Don't stand in the way of anything that happens to them as a result of their drinking.

This doesn't mean you have to stop caring for your loved one, quite the opposite actually. You need to re-examine your version of helping them. Your old ways were well-intentioned and compassionate but also deprived the alcohol dependent of opportunities to help themselves. Your motivation behind assisting them was probably also laced around stopping yourself from getting anxious, worried or stressed.

Now See What You've Done

Sometimes when we want our alcoholic partner to see the error of their ways, we try to speed the process up by highlighting what's happened as a result of their drinking, thereby making them feel guilty. Do not to be tempted to do this by creating crisis situations that make it harder for the alcoholic and equally, do not stand in the way if situations arise that could cause them to want to change.

The more you concentrate on you and any children you have and remain calm, the more the alcoholic will have to face what they are doing because they will not have you to blame for their drinking or actions. If you aren't fighting with them, pouring their drinks, covering for them or lying for them, they'll have to start looking at themselves.

It is not a cast iron guarantee but eventually, most alcohol dependents will see the devastation they've caused themselves and others and eventually seek help.

One thing is sure though, if you continue to stand in the way of them facing the full consequences of their actions, they are highly likely to continue drinking.

This doesn't mean you have to become selfish or uncaring but you will need to do everything in proportion. You can still care for your partner without wrapping them in a false protective layer. Think about the things you are doing for them that you wouldn't need to do if they were a normal, capable, sober human being.

The things you've chosen to take responsibility for are not really your responsibility. Leave your partner to do things such as getting undressed, calling their workplace and cleaning up after themselves. In other words, don't protect the drinker from the naturally occurring consequences of their drinking. If they embarrass themselves, don't make excuses for them and harder still, if they fall, don't pick them up.

For most people, this kind of tough love is an incredibly difficult thing to do; ignoring your loved one's actions when they are drunk goes very much against the grain. However, protecting the drinker means they never suffer the consequences and as a result, are never fully aware of the severity of their drinking.

Many believe that problem drinkers only seek help when they are hurting, when they can no longer bear the way they live, therefore, protecting the drinker only delays that time from arriving.

Exercise 3: Review

Look back at the list of your responsibilities in your notebook from Exercise 2. Now cross off the items on the list that are not your responsibility but actually the responsibility of your alcoholic loved one. These are things they would normally be capable of doing if they were sober, such as attending to their personal hygiene, cleaning up after themselves and making their own excuses where necessary.

Now put an X beside the items they would normally share with you if they were sober, such as sharing the washing up, tidying the house, cutting the lawn and so on.

Look at the items that are left on your list. It's probably a lot shorter and the items that remain are core daily responsibilities that in a normal life you would do.

From this point on, you are not going to allow yourself to do those crossed-off items. Additionally, don't instruct your partner to do the normal day-to-day things from your list that a normal functioning person would do. It is not your responsibility to tell another adult to perform these basic tasks.

When they are sober however, frequently ask them to do one of the items marked with an X. Don't ask repeatedly in any one session and don't pester, don't check up on whether they've done it, just ask in a way that shows you take it for granted that they will simply do it.

If you end up doing it yourself, don't make a big deal out of it. The idea is to begin to treat your alcoholic loved one in a normal way, without taking responsibility for their actions.

The journey of a thousand miles begins with a single step: Lao-tze

Alcoholics Anonymous defines insanity as continuing the same behaviour and expecting a different result. If your partner continues drinking, their life is only going to continue to yield the same results. The same goes for you. If you keep reacting to their drinking and continue to blame them for your resulting life, than your life is not going to get any better either.

Taking responsibility for the choices you make has an empowering energy. It takes two to tango and you are participating in a dance which isn't improving your life.

I was surprised to hear in rehab counselling that I was as sick as my husband. My mental illness was feeding off my reactions to his actions. I had been severely affected by alcohol without being the drunk. You too need to look at your own recovery and stop spending time reacting to your alcoholic's life decisions and wishing your life was different.

Don't feel guilty about the past; that was a time when you had neither the tools nor the strength to make a decision and follow it through. It was the best you could do under the circumstances and now you need to move forward.

Whilst you cannot change the past you can make amends and learn from mistakes. You need to define what you are responsible for and outline the values you want to live by.

Likewise, don't feel threatened by the future. By taking responsibility and changing your behaviour you will lead a more fulfilling and enjoyable life by taking one day at a time. Don't expect things to happen overnight but remember, by taking little steps every day which may be hardly noticeable, you will probably look back some day soon and say, 'Wow, look how far I've come!'

You will start to feel proud of the changes you have made to your home, work and family life and perhaps most importantly, to yourself.

Chapter 5

The U-Turn Back To You

Who Are You?
Can You Answer This Question?

During my early twenties I would have stood up and said:

'I'm an independent young woman who loves travelling and writing, who believes in living every day to its fullest and I have countless dreams which no one can stop me following'.

This was what I called my life expectation. By the time I reached rock bottom with my husband's drinking less than ten years later, I would have said:

'I'm a mother of two and the wife of an alcoholic who has given up struggling to pay my debts.

I had dreams but right now, I'd give anything for a normal life with a non-alcoholic partner.

I don't have the time to follow my dreams or even remember what they were; they probably weren't very practical anyway. Travel is a pain now as it's too stressful with an alcoholic partner in tow and I feel older than my years.

I envy my friends lives and feel bitter about the hand that God has dealt me. I like to retain a positive attitude for my children and put on a brave face to friends but sometimes this is so hard and as a result, I often avoid friends and family for as long as I can get away with.

Writing? I don't have time really and I don't have time to exercise or look after my health the way I used to, I'm too busy trying to sort other people's lives out, however, I feel I am a strong person.'

This was my real life description.

Exercise 4: Life Description

Summary of You: Read my real life description again and in your notebook write your present real life description. In ten lines summarise yourself, your lifestyle, how you view yourself and how you behave on a daily basis.

Now, think back to your life before your current situation when you were a teenager or young adult and remember how you wanted or hoped your future would be. Think about how you saw yourself and how you wanted other people to see you. In your notebook write five lines describing your life expectation and how you imagined your life would be.

Tired Of Living
Your Life Description?

I got very tired of living my real life description so I began to experiment with new ways of living, loving and thinking. As a result, I have completely changed my life and outlook and have returned to loving and living life to the fullest; now I am going to show you how to do the same.

As a result of four years of experimenting, my life description has changed again. I would now stand up and say, 'I'm a young mum of two in her thirties but I feel about ten years younger and am getting younger rather than older! My passions are my family, travelling, writing and living life to the full.

I cry laughing at least once a week if not more. I still have debts but managed to have four foreign holidays last year,

I completed my first novel and have a good relationship with my happy, healthy kids and loving husband and I don't let my responsibilities, such as my job, get in the way of taking care of myself.'

Did you notice how I no longer identified myself as the wife of an alcoholic? Actually, alcohol doesn't feature in any part of my life description. My husband is still an alcoholic, although not an active alcoholic, at the time of writing; I never take sobriety for granted.

There is far more to your identity than another person's disease. For example, if you found out a co-worker had cancer, would you prioritise your identity as being a co-worker of a cancer patient and therefore a victim of cancer? Being the co-worker of a cancer patient may be relevant if you were attending a support meeting or doing a fund-raising event for cancer services but generally it wouldn't form part of your identity.

The same applies to living with the effects that alcohol has on another person and unless you are in a support group meeting or counselling session, the fact that your spouse, partner, family member or friend is an alcoholic, is not part of your identity.

My husband is an important part of my life but I stopped his addiction being part of me and by doing so he became sober.

If your life description and identity has been lost and buried underneath an avalanche of problems and burdens, we'll need to look at why your life is in such disarray and has strayed so far from the path of your life expectation before we can take the first crucial steps to getting it back on track.

Chapter 6

Getting Out Of Isolation

When someone discovers they have an illness, friends and family members usually rally support from near and far. They take the kids, run errands, call regularly and more besides. Addiction is one of the most isolating diseases for the sufferer and more so for those who live with them. I say more so, because the sufferer usually buries their isolation in a bottle which helps them forget and can make years pass without the drinker caring about how anyone else feels.

People who live with an active alcoholic devote a lot of time and energy to hiding evidence of their problem. They spend time apologising for someone else's actions while the person who carried out the action may be oblivious to what they have done. They can't apologise enough to employers, co-workers, friends, other family members and relatives for bad behaviour that wasn't theirs.

Isolation kicks in as early as a few months into a serious drinking addiction and this isolation from friends, family and society in general, gradually takes over, although it can take years before you actually realise what's happening.

As the problem increases, contact with your social circles decreases in order to avoid difficult situations, shame and embarrassment. You might convince yourself that this apparent lack of contact is occurring for other reasons like you're too busy, you have drifted apart and so on.

Talking to someone about your feelings can help you feel less alone and they might be able to lift your spirits too; having friends and people to talk to is extremely important during your recovery.

Paranoia can creep in when you feel someone hasn't telephoned or stopped to talk to you because they know your secret and maybe the real reason they haven't asked you to their wedding is because they don't like you any more.

Other people's reactions can absorb us and eat away at our self-esteem. It's only in post-recovery that you're able to look back and see why people were like that. It's also easier to accept these people had lives with problems and challenges too and your alcohol tainted existence may have affected your behaviour towards them.

If you've lost friends due to embarrassment caused by your loved one's behaviour, it's high time to start making amends with old friends and/or making a few new ones.

If you had friendships that were near and dear to you that have gone by the wayside, take some time out to examine the reasons why. They often fall into one of the following three categories:

Same Friends: You socialised together with your alcoholic loved one as part of a group but your alcoholic partner began to drink too much and became obnoxious, aggressive, sick, or an unwanted responsibility for the rest of the group. Consequently, the invitations to go out began to decrease over time.

Solution: Become an independent socialiser. A key element to making this work is to stop having secrets. If these people were your friends they probably recognised that your partner had a drinking problem which ended up ruining everyone's enjoyment, before you were ready to admit they had a drinking problem.

If your friends still go out socialising together, consider giving them a call, acknowledge how bad your partner's behaviour was at times and ask them to contact you the next time they are planning to meet up and suggest that you go too, without your partner.

It might feel awkward at first but you'll soon be recognised as a person in your own right, not just half of a couple. The invitations are likely to return for you as an independent socialiser and this will help to bring you out of your isolation.

A word of caution; be careful not to talk about your problems while you're out. Use these events as a complete break away from your daily issues. Even if a friend asks about your partner, do not discuss them, no matter how tempting it is to do so.

Just say you don't want to talk about it at that point and perhaps suggest you could have a chat about it on the phone during the week; wait for them to call you, don't pro-actively arrange to have that conversation.

You Have Grown Apart: Even the best of friends move on with their lives. Imagine one person gets married and has kids, while the other is single and doing a Master's degree, or partying their way around the world; it can be difficult for them to relate to each other's trials, tribulations, challenges and joys.

Some of your friends may have moved on in such a way that the differences between you might be so large, it's difficult to find any common ground.

Solution: Send birthday and Christmas cards. Send the odd e-mail or stay in touch through a social network such as Facebook or Twitter.

In time, your lives might level out and you might even rediscover those common threads that unlock happy memories of old times.

Burn Out: Your friends never phone any more, or return your calls.

Solution: Think about the last series of meetings or telephone calls you had with them. Did you cry, complain, grumble, moan and pour your heart out? Indeed, that is what friends are for, to share the good times and help each other through the bad, but give a thought to the balance of good and bad.

Do you recall any major problems your friends shared with you, can you remember the details or how often you called to ask how things were going for them? Can you remember the balance with clarity?

The fact is you probably can't and if your life was chaotic at the time, there's a strong possibility that you called these friends on a regular basis to offload how your partner was behaving. I imagine they offered an ear for the first few times and offered solutions or advice during others that included get them to rehab, don't put up with it any more or simply leave them.

You probably listened but didn't take their advice or want their advice and instead continued with the same behaviour pattern, using their ears to vent your frustrations and emotions.

Another typical scenario may have found you using their home as an occasional place of sanctuary or refuge and you swearing to them that you'd never go back to live with your alcoholic partner. During these distressing times, your friends may well have sacrificed hours of their time supplying you with tissues and a comforting ear.

Did you leave them? If yes, I guess you went back too or you wouldn't be reading this and when that friend called again, you probably brushed over everything, saying things were different now, you knew how to change things, you were in control and so on.

There are a limited number of times even a good friend can hear this, without withdrawing their company and/or their friendship.

Everyone has challenges in their lives. Your friend may have had problems they didn't want to burden you with because you already had enough going on in your own life. Perhaps they reached their limits with their issues and didn't want to have to re-listen to your problems over and over again.

The first step to rekindling and repairing this type of highly tested, dwindled friendship is to learn how to listen. That might sound easy but it's far more difficult than you think.

Chapter 7

Listening

From your extensive experience of living with an alcoholic partner, your mind will have become used to racing ahead. You probably try to live ten steps ahead of the action you think they are likely to take and prepare yourself with a variety of reactions to suit different scenarios each day.

It's quite exhausting to be constantly thinking ahead, rather than living in the moment and as a result, you may find you cannot give anyone or anything 100% of your attention; unfortunately, that is one of the pre-requisites for listening.

I learned how to listen in rehab after-care, which consisted of a weekly meeting for addicts and their partners. We agreed to attend them for a two-year period following my husband's stay in rehab. Each week, everyone at the meeting had an opportunity to talk about their week and how they coped with different situations.

It was easy to spot the new people in the group as they were either staring off into space thinking about their problems or dying to talk about themselves so much that they couldn't contribute to what the rest of the group was saying; they weren't listening.

Gradually, they began to realise it was a safe and secure place to discuss their ups and downs and their worries and joys.

With time and patience, we all learned to listen to the rest of the group and share in what everyone had to say. Before joining the group I would always have been the first to jump in with a solution, or to offer advice that began with, 'Do you know what you should do...?' However, these group meetings taught me that I don't have to be the one to find a solution to everyone's problems, or to be the judge of how they are dealing with their situations.

Once you stop trying to predict how things will probably work out in every situation, it will be easier to pay attention to what you are doing and to hear what other people are saying.

Initially, you may be like I was and when people offer you advice, a voice in your head says, 'They don't understand!' Unless someone has lived with alcohol, it is indeed difficult for them to understand which is why rehab groups and Al-Anon groups are terrific support systems.

If you turn to them for help, you'll find yourself surrounded by people who have been through the same experiences as you. They offer listening support which enables you to figure out the best way forward, for you.

If you don't think a friend understands your situation or can give you productive advice, don't talk to them about that part of your life. Talk to them about the children, your job, your co-workers, your dreams, everything else but your partner and your relationship; save that for your Al-Anon meetings.

If you know someone who is helpful and you respect their advice, replace your complaining with requests for advice and listen to it intently. If you feel deep down what they're saying is the right course of action for you, follow that advice!

There is absolutely no point in grumbling about your situation as it solves nothing without follow-up action. Ultimately, it's up to you to make a change and do something different.

Chapter 8

Quality Time

It's time to push yourself to live your life another way. Making friends isn't easy as an adult, especially if your guard is up and your self-esteem is knocked down from living with such a big secret.

I've talked about the Al-Anon groups but a positive step forward would be for you to actually attend a meeting. They are used day and night, all around the world by non-judgemental, ordinary people just like you. You'll reap the benefits of taking part in their sessions and see increased self-confidence and when you're feeling down, alone, isolated or angry, you can pick up the phone and call somebody from your group who will help you through the tough times.

Once you are feeling a little more confident, push yourself to go out each day. Perhaps consider getting a part-time job, join a parent and toddler group, become a volunteer at a local charity shop, go back to school or maybe take a night class.

Heed my advice from the previous chapter and don't tell your life story to the first person you befriend, remember other people have their own problems and lives too. Use opportunities with new friends or colleagues to explore the positive parts of your personality and use your Al-Anon meetings, or a close family member to talk about your issues with your partner's drinking.

Blogging

If you have a computer with Internet access, another way to vent your frustrations and share with people who may understand, is through blogging or participating in chat rooms. You can set up your own blog free of charge by using a system such as Blogger.com or WordPress.com.

Bloggers write entries on their website on a regular basis for anyone to read but they can also limit who is allowed to read their posts. The readership can even be by invitation only if the blogger chooses. Some bloggers are experts in specialist fields, others are regular people just like you and I, experiencing and dealing with their day-to-day lives, then sharing their thoughts with the world at large.

You can blog anonymously if you wish and it is a great way to express your thoughts and feelings and get things off your chest. If you are computer illiterate, you may have just identified the perfect night school course for you!

However, sitting at the computer blogging or participating in chat rooms every day, cannot replace the necessity to get involved in outside activities which will help you forget about the problems at home for a while and help you develop some self-respect.

Call To Action!

This weekend go out somewhere for two hours without your partner. Maybe have a walk on a beach or through a park. Don't do it with conditions and don't call to check up on them. Don't do it as an act or by making a big statement like, 'Now I'll show them'. Do it for you. Think about the good things in your life and don't allow negative thoughts to take over.

Golden Key Three

Enjoying Your Own Company

Make a solid commitment to go on an outing or take a pleasure walk each weekend. If you have kids, make it part of their weekend routine. It doesn't have to be a major event, a couple of hours will suffice.

While you're getting ready to go out, invite your partner to go with you, if they are sober. If they don't want to go, accept their decision and don't try to press-gang them into going with you. Remember, you are doing this for yourself and any children, not for the alcoholic.

This is another little step designed to help you take more responsibility for yourself and the other non-addicted people around you. If the alcoholic in your life wishes to get involved, that's fine, if not, that's fine too.

Remember you can do things together, as well as with others, or on your own.

Making Plans

In the past I imagine your alcoholic partner has probably let you down a lot on the subject of making plans for outings, events, holidays and so on. Do not make plans around your partner any longer. Make plans for you and your children, or you and a friend and just go off and have some fun.

Without your partner involved, you no longer have to

worry about whether the outing is going to be just another day that they are going to ruin.

Your partner isn't purposely trying to destroy their own life, they are sick and you can help them want to get well by allowing them to realise they are missing out on valuable precious time with you and the family. This realisation will not happen immediately but usually does with time.

When you are at your event or planned outing, don't waste time preparing what you are going to tell them when you get home. If they ask about it, talk about it, but don't force the information upon them, just relax and enjoy your time away from the house and gradually your positive behaviour will speak volumes.

This is a far better method of evoking change than you making them feel guilty or left out. Lasting change probably won't happen overnight but it will happen.

Time Out Alone

When you spend more time out with friends be it going to an adult education class or an Al-Anon meeting, you may find yourself accused by your alcoholic partner of not caring, having an affair, or simply not being there when they need you.

These accusations may be levelled at you because your new behaviour is challenging their comfort zone; you are the security blanket to their addiction and you are now threatening that security.

Alcoholism also causes paranoia and their unbalanced mind will create all sorts of reasons why you shouldn't go out and you shouldn't change. All levels of guilt will be placed upon your shoulders for leaving the house for an hour or so, to be an adult.

Additionally, they may tell you all the things that occurred while you were out and wax lyrical about how great they were dealing with it. It's just the everyday stuff that you deal with all the time, but to them it's a big deal because they wanted or needed to prove to you that they're a responsible adult without you. All of which is fine, just don't make a big deal out of it, let them talk.

When we change things we experience something new, different and unknown and because of that, we are frequently reticent and afraid of the change to some degree, but do your best to stick with your new plan and keep at it.

If you accept that the only person in the problematic relationship you can change is you and also that you are willing to make an effort in order to effect a positive change, you are hereby giving yourself the power to radically alter the direction of your entire life.

Chapter 9

Your Mental Health

You've probably tried a variety of ways to get through to your partner, including using sarcasm, sneers and clever verbal attacks. You may have spent hours rehearsing what you are going to say, polishing those cutting words to such an extent they will surely sink so deep they could never be forgotten, no matter how drunk your partner was.

You may be surprised how nasty you can become at times, feeling almost as guilty as the alcoholic does when they sober up and recall their behaviour. You might even have lashed out at them physically, which only fills you with shame and regret at how bad a person you've become.

This is not how you wanted to treat the love of your life and it certainly wasn't part of the fairy tale happiness you hoped for at the start of your relationship. As a result of all of this dark inner turbulence, you might not like yourself very much right now.

Exercise 5: Negativity

Write a list of adverbs that describe you. Underline the negative ones and highlight the positive ones. When you've completed it, look back over your negative list. Have you used words such as stupid, lazy, critical and boring? Now ask yourself, would you ever use these terms to describe a friend? Probably not, in fact I imagine you'd have to dislike the person a great deal to describe them in such harsh and negative terms.

Stop beating yourself up and start treating yourself the same way you would a best friend, then double it! None of us are perfect, that's a fact of life, but you'll only be able to recover from the damage you've done to yourself from living with alcoholism by treating yourself with absolute love and approval.

Dealing With Your Own Anger

Anger is a powerful emotion and it is important to vent it but not in a way that leaves you filled with regret.

When you feel the need to lash out, it's time to call someone from your support group, go for a walk or do something that relaxes you and removes you from the negative situation.

Take the dog or children out and go to the park, or call a good friend and meet up somewhere for a coffee. The more you keep the situation in control and the less you fight with the alcoholic, the more they will come to realise that it's their behaviour and not yours, that causes them to drink. They will begin to own their behaviour, just as you are starting to own yours.

You know now that you cannot control their behaviour and it is not your responsibility to do so either. The only thing you can do is control how you respond to their drinking and no response, is often the best response.

Call To Action!

The next time raging anger bubbles up inside you and you feel as though you need to vent a humiliating tirade on your alcoholic partner, focus every cell in your body on resolving the bigger problem and calmly walk away from the situation.

Get a pen and paper and write every nasty thing you want to say to them. Writing is a great way of venting your anger in a positive and acceptable way. Once you've written it all out, you can burn the piece of paper that carries all those vitriolic words and be proud of how you dealt with the human being in your life, rather than feel ashamed of your own behaviour.

If possible or appropriate, find a time when the person is sober and communicate with them in a calm and constructive manner. 95% of what an alcoholic says when they are inebriated is manipulative and hogwash anyway. Don't start believing in the lies of the disease, even if the lies include hopeful messages such as, 'I'm never drinking again!'

Don't try to convince your partner to stop drinking when they are drunk. Separate yourself from the antics of the alcoholic. The more time you spend looking out for your own well-being and not responding to them in anger, the healthier you and your children will become.

If you stay on track with my advice, your house won't be filled with the chaos you have lived with for so long and it will be calmer.

No matter what the alcoholic does, it will not affect you the way it did before and although you are allowed to be sympathetic when they get into trouble, you will no longer try to solve their problems, because you will be too busy taking care of your responsibilities to worry about them.

It Takes Time

Do not expect things to happen overnight. It has taken both you and your partner a long time to dig the hole this deep and it may well take the same time and energy to fill it back in so you can achieve a level playing field.

Don't have expectations of how your alcoholic partner is going to react to the way you are changing and the ways you are correcting your behaviour to achieve the life of your dreams. This process can take weeks, months or even years.

The pattern usually follows similar stages to these:

1. You start to make changes in your behaviour.

2. The alcoholic protests, bullies and tries to control you as they want to stay in their comfort zone.

3. You continue to grow in self-confidence and independence and are less affected by their behaviour.

4. The alcoholic sulks and alters their behaviour tactics to try to control you.

5. You begin to enjoy elements of your new behaviour. You are now detached but still love your alcoholic partner.

6. The alcoholic becomes afraid as they see themselves losing control of the situation and life isn't as easy as it used to be. They also come to realise they have a problem and are unhappy with their lifestyle.

7. You continue to be detached and don't exercise control of their life choices.

8. The alcoholic gets fed up with their lifestyle and the results of their behaviour, otherwise known as rock bottom.

9. They start to look for ways to change their behaviour.

10. You support their efforts and continue with your independence.

This is your path to self-improvement and if your alcoholic partner chooses to follow one too, that's their choice. If they decide not to, there is nothing you can do about it, but at the end of the path you can look back at how far you've progressed and how much your life has improved.

If all else fails and your alcohol dependent partner continues to drink and not accept responsibility for the problems they are causing, you may have to consider other alternatives.

If you've been taking care of yourself and your home is indeed calmer, you'll be in a far better state of mind to decide your future than if you were still immersed in the conditions you have been living in for so long.

It is almost impossible for us to make the right decisions when acting out of fear or desperation. We cannot change the alcoholic but we can change ourselves and the way we react to their drinking.

Do Not Indulge Yourself

Sometimes we adopt coping strategies to help ourselves get through difficult times, such as working or eating excessively. Work can give us a sense of mastery and fulfilment, along with much needed money of course and eating can be a source of comfort and pleasure, as well as a way to fuel ourselves.

Work and comfort eating can also be used to numb or avoid painful feelings and situations in ways that might ultimately be counter-productive. If you have indulged yourself in work or food as a coping mechanism, you will need to address this issue in due course.

When you are in a painful relationship which you don't want to walk away from, for whatever reason, it is important to take control of your own happiness in ways that do not include excesses of work, food or drink.

Try to enlarge your life beyond your partner, your job and food by adding new dimensions to it that might enrich what now feels impoverished and painful.

The choice of new activities of course, depends on what best suits you. It could be a new hobby or two, taking an adult education class in something that has always interested or inspired you, socialising with friends, hiking, reading or whatever works for you. Of course, counselling or life coaching could also help you address your issues and help you explore your options.

Don't Join Them

There is a common saying and it's also a trap that many of us fall into; 'If you can't beat 'em, join 'em.'

Whatever you do, don't join in and drink along with the drinker. It might seem like a natural thing to do but it just makes the drinking behaviour appear to be normal, which of course it is not. Besides, if you do try and you manage to keep up with them, it could result in you needing help too and one alcohol dependent is more than enough for any household.

Depression

After living with a chronic alcoholic for a few years, many people become depressed. Their life can become a permanent burden with few or no moments of authentic joy and comfort.

Apathy, aversion, physical pain and chronic fatigue may be common bodily expressions for you during this process. Expectations of these inevitable huge dips become the norm, following empty promises of sobriety and incalculable periods between their drinking binges.

Each dip can be more gut-wrenching than the last and we often form a mental barrier to stop ourselves being hurt. We become emotionally numb which reduces the heartache and sadness these dips bring, but also dulls the joy and laughter of happy times. The net result of this limits us to experiencing a range of bland, watered-down emotions.

Golden Key Four

Transcendental Meditation

Life with an alcoholic is like a road trip, full of hills and valleys, surprises, manoeuvres, abruptness and instability within the relationship that causes a constant shaking to your nervous system.

When a person experiences a serious trauma, they can be filled with a sense of excitement. This happens because when the body experiences shock, adrenaline is thrown into the bloodstream and adrenaline causes euphoria.

If you're struggling with depression you may be unconsciously searching for situations to keep you in an excited state. It is important to recognise this and to start looking for ways to help keep your emotions more stable, but still allowing you to enjoy the highs that life presents.

The daily practice of Transcendental Meditation relaxes the mind and helps stabilise your emotions. Without it, my husband would not have stayed sober and I wouldn't have got through what I did quite so well.

Seek out an Ayurvedic centre or a Transcendental Meditation teacher near you and find out more about these amazing relaxation techniques.

Denial

A common trait of alcoholics is denial. Denial that they have a problem and denial that their drinking causes any major problems. However, partners of alcoholics also often live in denial.

Despite all evidence to the contrary, we insist that our efforts to keep the peace, making life bearable for all involved, are working. Indeed, we make ourselves believe that our situation isn't all that bad.

Stop defending your position and maintaining your current life because doing even more of something that you know doesn't work, won't make your life better!

You have to recognise the problem for what it is and decide to change things, in much the same way as the alcoholic has to change their behaviour.

Denial can be born out of a fear of change and that something far worse might happen if we admit how bad things have become, forcing us to take action.

Other people often recognise the seriousness of a problem before the person living with it on a daily basis does. For many it's a case of not being able to see the wood for the trees.

After you have faced up to a major problem like this and worked your way through it, any other challenges you come up against in life will seem like a piece of cake!

Being The Martyr

Whenever anyone asked me how I was, I always answered, 'Fine, how are you?' Inside however, I was a crumbling mess. I didn't listen to their replies as I was too concerned about how they were perceiving me.

I am not advocating that while you are chatting in the middle of the street or supermarket you should answer, 'Actually, I'm an emotional mess and my life is falling apart'. That would be a bit of a conversation stopper.

However, you do need an outlet where you can be honest with yourself when someone asks how you are. Al-Anon is that perfect place. The service they offer is confidential and meetings are held in many secure locations that you should be able to attend once or twice a week.

Al-Anon Meetings

I cannot emphasise enough the benefits of Al-Anon. You can go to a meeting anywhere in the world and be assured that the group will not be promoting affiliation to any therapies, religion, political party or anything else for that matter. The only membership requirement you need is to have encountered a problem of alcohol addiction in a relative or friend.

Chapter 10

Making Room For Change

It's time to prepare for change. You need to make room in your head, mind and heart for yourself and your new life. If you are distracted by chaos and clutter, you will not be able to stay strong and focused.

Clean up your incompletions and tidy up any messy ends so you can make room for opportunity and abundance to come into your life.

By taking time to clean out old physical and mental clutter from drawers, spare rooms, under beds, filing cabinets, wardrobes and your heart and mind, you'll enjoy better mental health and be able to deal with difficult issues with a clearer, calmer disposition.

Clutter In Your Head And Heart

You probably like to give the appearance to outsiders that you are a great person who can always be relied upon to be happy, upbeat and available to help anyone, even though you probably have burdens of your own to deal with.

Some partners of alcoholics derive comfort from hearing statements like, 'You're great, I don't know how you do it' and so on. The attention and pity people give you because of your suffering, probably makes you feel good.

A large part of your identity might come from the way other people observe how you cope with your suffering. You are not alone in this, indeed many of us have fallen into this trap. We did it with such elegance too, we were heroes for the cause and saints in the making.

However, friendly claps on the back for getting on with life, is not to be commended. Don't allow yourself to miss out on life any more.

When you play out the role of a hero, you close your eyes to your disadvantages and your own weakness. You might also place a focus on befriending people whose problems seem far worse than yours that also require radical solutions.

You may feel as though you attract chaos, however by getting involved with volatile people in chaotic, uncertain and emotionally disadvantaged situations, you avoid thoughts of responsibility for your own life.

Furthermore, by getting involved in other people's dramatic problems you can comfortably ignore addressing your own issues and avoid making practical decisions concerning important aspects of your own life.

Looking good on the outside and ignoring our true feelings on the inside doesn't work for long. We get on with the business of helping control others, but in doing so, we keep everyone else at a comfortable distance.

This is safe behaviour. You may feel that if you don't let them past your barrier, you won't have to acknowledge the pain you're feeling inside. You might even believe you can maintain this happy veneer and get through your days imagining that you're making the most of the hand you've been dealt; it's a fallacy.

By not sharing your true feelings with an understanding friend or group and continuing to be a do-gooder, you are not actually achieving anything. If you call a halt to looking after everyone else's problems and start to be true to yourself, you will begin to experience real communication, real relationships and real happiness.

It's time to learn how to say 'No' to people who are using you to sort out their problems.

Exercise 6: Responsibility

Make a list of the people you feel you have hurt, rejected or harmed in the past as a result of your circumstances. Your list may include anyone that you feel you have disappointed too. When you compile your list, bear in mind that no one else needs to know who is on it, so be truthful.

Examples could include people like your parents, who might be on the list because they expected you to go to university but you didn't. Or your child, because you didn't let them have that tattoo. Or maybe a close friend, because you didn't lend them money.

Be careful here and remember you are not responsible for everyone's unfulfilled needs or desires, so these situations shouldn't be included on your list.

You are not responsible for the operations of other people, places or things but you are responsible for your own actions.

Do you think you may have an exaggerated sense of responsibility? You must remember, we can only do so much and the choices we make for ourselves, may be uncomfortable or unacceptable to others.

With this new perspective firmly planted in your mind, you might want to revise and cross some of those people off your initial list.

You do not need to take care of everything and everybody and you do have a personal choice in the matter.

Once you have a definitive list, think of ways to make amends to the people on it. This repairing of relationships can be done over time, once you feel a little stronger.

There are elements in our lives that we all need to deal with, they are our responsibility. However, if we want to achieve different results from our lives, we need to make ourselves our primary responsibility.

Remember the oxygen mask I talked about at the beginning of the book? You need to make your own mental and emotional health your primary responsibility, before you can help others.

Numb

Disappointment can make you feel numb so much so that you begin to operate on automatic. You behave like a robot; you function, you get through the day, you do what is expected of you and say what is expected of you. Your face, actions and voice show little expression. You shut off your dreams and stop expecting happiness in life.

I remember realising this and telling myself to stop feeling sorry for myself. I felt I should accept that this was what real life was about, this was what being a responsible grown up was all about and that dreams and excitement were childish things.

The eventual realisation that I was operating on automatic was probably my mind screaming at me to wake up but my barrier wanted to stop me feeling the agony of perpetual disappointment. By stopping myself from expecting happiness or joy, I couldn't be let down or disappointed any more. I was taking the less risky path.

Thankfully, I had a strong mind that didn't want to accept the mundane yet chaos-ridden path. My mind knew that I had the potential to feel great happiness as well as enormous sadness and that I could deal with both.

By acknowledging that life is indeed a series of ups and downs, I stopped the fear of disappointment preventing me from feeling happy.

Finding Happiness

Once you've stopped trying to control the future and started to actually feel your feelings as they happen, you will begin to truly live in the moment.

By doing so, you won't ever miss precious moments of happiness or joy that were previously overlooked because you were too busy dealing with the serious drink related issues of the day.

When you experience moments of happiness and joy, don't try to hold on to them or attempt to make time stand still. Like all emotions, joy and happiness flow like the tides and just like water, you cannot grip or hold them.

However, you can enjoy the sensation of them when they're present and when they leave, you'll need to get on with other things until the next tide comes in.

While we're waiting for the next big splashes to arrive, we can seek out little rock pools and create our own mini-splashes of happiness!

Happiness isn't solely created by large events such as getting the car you always wanted, going on an amazing holiday or paying off your mortgage. Snippets of joy can be found in regular daily events that you may have overlooked before, things like new life in the garden, news of a pregnancy, even a rainbow in the middle of a storm.

Happiness does not come from outer things or other people, it comes from within. By learning to take responsibility for your own actions and changing your expectations of others, you will stop feeling deprived of life's glories and start creating your own.

Taking little steps along this path will stop you feeling sorry for yourself and you'll start creating situations that will develop an appreciation for yourself and your own strengths.

Call to Action!

Start your day by sending gratitude to the Universe or your God. List ten things you are grateful for, examples may include your health, the children, your musical abilities, a roof over your head, friends or your faithful dog.

Golden Key Five

Daily Moment of Happiness

Discipline yourself to find a moment of happiness and an appreciation of life every day no matter how fleeting it is. Work at this and do not allow yourself to feel like a helpless victim with nothing to be happy about. Remember, happiness comes from within, so without your effort, happiness will not be created within you.

Begin to look for additional things in your everyday life that you could appreciate and enjoy more than you currently do. It might come from contributing a comment or two to a light conversation with a co-worker, petting your dog or cat, looking at the amazing intricate make-up of a flower, paying somebody a genuine compliment, splashing your child during bath time or reading them a story at bedtime.

For a spirit that is broken, this can require an enormous effort, however, by starting to appreciate the small blessings of life, you will make room in your heart for happiness, which holds the key to the healing process.

Chapter 11

Destructive Words

When somebody insults or criticises you, or points out faults they believe you have, it can make you feel low enough to start believing them.

Alcoholics often do this to the people they love. If someone tells you that you have two heads for long enough, you might actually start to believe it.

One person's version of reality might not be correct which is why it's important to reach out to others and explore the limiting beliefs this person has made you feel about yourself. By doing so, you can cast off negative views you have of yourself and start exploring who you really are.

Gossip

When we have been berated by cruel words over a long period of time, it can be all too easy for us to do the same to others. For a short period, behaving this way can make us feel better about ourselves.

It's easy to become obsessed with other people's problems and drama and by talking about them to others, our own life problems can seem trivial. It can give us comfort to think that other people's lives aren't perfect either. I'm talking about gossip, generally spread by those who have a low opinion of themselves.

Criticism

Stop taking on board ignorant behaviour, harsh words and insults that are levelled at you by your loved one when they are drinking. Will they remember what they've said when they sober up? Probably not, so why should you take notice of what they had to say? It was drink-fuelled and you must let these words flow over you like the proverbial water off the duck's back.

Experiencing other people's limiting and negative behaviour does not mean we have to drop our standards. By taking responsibility for your actions and words and changing your behaviour for the better, you'll begin to form another part of yourself that you can be proud of. This has a huge knock-on effect too because you'll also start to feel good about yourself and that is an immensely powerful step forward in your healing process.

People who feel genuinely good about themselves no longer feel the need to assault other people's characters and this includes the alcoholic partner. Criticism and insults never make a situation better, they only serve to make people feel worse and guilty. For an alcoholic, this can lead to them wanting to block out the guilt, so they continue to drink.

When you start to feel tension building, it's important to do all you can to stop it escalating and turning into something which is a lot harder to handle. By sharing your problem with a trusted contact from your Al-Anon group, you can disperse your tension and if you haven't got that far yet, just write it down.

Writing about how you feel is a great way of pouring the negative thoughts out of your head and it can stop the situation from turning into high drama with an onslaught of cruel words.

Exercise 7: Criticism

Make a list of your alcoholic loved one's limitations including all the things you regularly tell them they do wrong, large and small. Note down everything you've criticised them for and nagged them about. You could probably take several hours and fill a dozen notebooks doing this, so you might like to set a time limit.

Now I'd like you to list your limitations. Write down all the chores you haven't got around to doing, or have actively put off and include any mistakes you've made in the last month.

Maybe your alcoholic loved one points these out to you and criticises you for them. How do you feel when that happens? If criticising isn't their thing, think about how you would feel if someone picked on you about your shortcomings on a regular basis. You'd feel pretty bad, wouldn't you?

Nothing has ever improved as a result of insulting, non-constructive criticism, and that is why you have to stop doing it to your loved one. All it does is focus your mind on their actions or inactions, rather than concentrating on your own self-improvement.

Criticism is a way of trying to exert power or control over another person's actions or attitude which only ever results in bitterness, frustration and hopelessness.

You must realise and accept that you do not have control over any other person's thoughts or actions. You can't stop anybody insulting or criticising you, but by recognising your own shortcomings and working on them, you can set foot on the road towards your own peace of mind.

Call To Action!

The next time you feel a burning criticism about to erupt from within you, bite your tongue! Distract yourself and think a positive thought about yourself instead.

Chapter 12

Courage To Change

This is your life and no one else can change it but you. You are an adult, you can make your own decisions and stop falling back on excuses or living in denial. You have to take control of your life and do something about it and you have made a great start by reading this book.

Make a conscious decision to take steps towards feeling good again. Do you remember feeling really good, feeling relaxed and not on edge all the time?

You'll find your reactions to receiving verbal abuse and disappointment fascinating and they change completely once you've become determined to feel good again.

It's as if the more you learn and concentrate on becoming the person you want to be, the less upset and anxious you become about impending bad behaviour and it also becomes easier to stop letting it affect you.

If you accept that you can have a satisfactory life without your partner meeting your expectations, you will stop feeling the need to treat them badly or like a child any more. Sometimes we have to accept alcoholism for the disease that it is and show compassion; it is OK to do this.

By developing yourself and growing stronger on the inside, you'll be better prepared to make a decision about whether you want to stay with your partner and you'll no longer feel miserable as you'll be in charge of your own life decisions.

It is crucially important that you stop battling and attempting to change external forces and that you stop fearing change and start to look within. Stop trying to change the things you cannot change. Change what you can and leave the rest; by doing this you will obtain your goals far quicker than you ever imagined.

Life Aims

There is absolutely no point in wasting your time and wishing your life away. You need to gracefully accept that this is your life and then get busy living it.

In order for your life to amount to more than an existence, it is important that you identify and articulate precisely what your life aims are. Life aims form a crucial part of your inner-most driving force. They give you a sense of direction and purpose and motivate you to your highest levels of energy.

Your life aims help you to lead a life that's consistent with your core values and beliefs and are the essential starting blocks for your new life. They are already there, deep within you, but like a great many people, you might not even realise they exist.

Imagine your life was a business. Now think about the greatest Managing Directors and CEOs of the world. They are ordinary people with an exceptionally dedicated focus for where they're going and how to get there. Great leaders also have a crystal clear vision of what they want from their world and they breathe life into that vision every day.

They work to maintain and reinforce their life aims and never give in to the idea of simply existing. I want you to work on your life aims every day and to stop just existing. It's time to recognise that every day of your life is precious.

Start living your life intentionally, rather than randomly. The way to create your dream life starts by looking at how you want to be in your whole life and it all begins with you realising your life aims.

Identifying Your Life Aims

You need to forget about your present daily life and think about how you'd like it to be. Remember, your daily actions are a means to support your primary focus and identifying your life aims is now your primary focus.

Ask yourself the following probing questions and write the answers down in your notebook. You'll be using the answers like a springboard which will encourage you to write more about your essence and purpose in life.

Here are a few questions to get you started but feel free to add any others you feel drawn to explore.

1. What do I want in my life?
2. What don't I want in my life?
3. How do I want my life to run on a day-to-day basis?
4. What would I like to be doing two years from now?
5. Ten years from now?
6. Twenty years from now?
7. What hobby have I always wanted to do?
8. What have I always wanted to study or work at?
9. Of all the things in my life, what has given me the most satisfaction or pleasure?
10. If I had everything I'd ever wanted, what would get me out of bed in the morning?

There is no such thing as a right or wrong life aim. Understanding them gives you the ability to live your life intentionally, rather than randomly. It also helps you make conscious choices in your actions and in your life, choices that are consistent with what you've identified is most important to you.

Doing so will help you set out your priorities and will help you to put your reactions to your partner's addiction in proper perspective.

Successful people don't waste time in denial, or complain and make excuses for that matter. They face their situations like a warrior. They look for the warning signs, find out why things aren't working, then solve the problems with hard work and by avoiding unnecessary risk and uncertainty.

Life will always be a series of challenges and choices and you get to decide what will move you closer to your life aims and goals, or farther away from them. External forces will always be part of the equation, even during the good times when your world is thriving.

Sometimes recognising the things that are not working in your life can be painful but at the same time a very powerful aid to helping you shape the life you want.

Don't try to rationalise the things that aren't working for you or make excuses for them or hide them. This is a time when it's important to take a personal inventory and evict all the excuses, bad rationalisations and hidden habits that don't serve you.

These things will keep you away from the life you want to live, if you let them.

Chapter 13

Can We Change?
Yes We Can!

By now you'll have realised the only person you can change is yourself. If you make a radical personal change, your relationship with your partner will also undoubtedly change too.

This dawning realisation gives you huge power over your life. New changes to your lifestyle will not be welcomed by your partner initially. They will probably view your actions as disturbing the norm they've been satisfied to go on with, to feed their need.

Their insecurities will be heightened because you will no longer be following their lead. Making changes takes courage, strength and renewed self-esteem and the road ahead might seem steep but you can get up it by taking little steps.

It may surprise you to know that simply deciding what you want is often the first and most important step to acquiring it. Our brain is a goal-seeking organ, in fact, scientists have found that the brain uses an activating system to filter the millions of images, sounds, impressions and messages we receive each day, delivering only what our conscious mind needs to survive and meet the goals we've identified.

When you decide what you want, you instruct your brain to start looking for information, opportunities and other resources to achieve it and if your life is to have any meaning beyond your partner's addiction, you must connect with what is most important to you.

Your daily actions should be making a healthy contribution to the realisation of the dream that started this adventure. It was that dream life you envisaged for yourself when you fell in love with your partner, or perhaps it occurred before you even met and fell in love.

If you've lost your way and are unclear about what that dream life is any more, how can you possibly set a course to find it?

Achieving success isn't easy, in fact, there's a tremendous amount of hard work that goes into it but one thing we know successful people do is stay positive about their hopeful, eventual outcome. They keep their eyes on the prize no matter what's going on around them and they stay focused on their goals.

Goals

There's an enormous difference between pretending everything's positive and taking action towards achieving a more positive future.

An effective life-changing exercise I came across some time ago was about goal setting, as laid out in a book called *The Success Principles* by Jack Canfield. I followed his instructions and wrote out my goals in detail. They weren't loose ideas or wishes, they were detailed specifics and I added a time-line too.

Instead of saying I want to earn more money, I wrote that I wanted an income of 1,000 Euros per week. Instead of asking for the house of my dreams, I asked for an old country house beside a river surrounded by mature trees and an old mill wall. Instead of stating that I wanted my husband to give up drink, I said I wanted him to have a fulfilling life, to be healthy, content and happy.

There were about twenty-five things on my list and for about six months, I read over them twice a day and then my notebook got lost. Two years later while unpacking my old bedside locker after a house move, I found my notebook stuck at the back of a drawer. I read over my goals with fond memories and realised to my amazement, that most of them had come to fruition.

My subconscious mind had been working away behind the scenes and slowly but surely without me even realising it, I'd achieved some of my goals; scuba diving with my kids, having four holidays a year, going on an adventure trip for myself to be a cowgirl and I had the income of 1,000 Euros per week. Incidentally, I was unpacking my locker after moving into my new home which was an old farmhouse with a river border mature woodland and an old mill wall.

I haven't yet reached my ideal weight, nor have I penned that best seller yet but there's still time!

None of my goals were about my husband being sober. That was out of my control and I knew it. However, as I progressed towards my goals, I was becoming the person I wanted to be. My husband saw me changing, becoming more confident and he knew if he didn't get his act together he would lose me, so he had to change. He had reached his rock bottom and he wanted to change. He is now living a fulfilling life and he is healthy, content, happy and best of all, he's sober.

Golden Key Six

Set Your Goals

Make a list of all the goals you want to achieve in life, no matter how strange or unlikely and don't let logic kick in.

Read it aloud in the morning and before you go to sleep at night. Concentrate on it and without any other effort, you will find subtle changes happening in your life which will lead you towards fulfilling your goals.

Think very carefully about your wording, be exact and specific. Instead of stating that you want your partner to get sober, think about why you want them sober and what the end result could be.

Consider rewording that wish along the lines of wanting to have a sober, caring, loving partner who will respect and love you and bring you breakfast in bed every Sunday morning by June two years hence.

As you progress with your other goals, your partner may well fall in line and become sober and turn into that loving partner.

Alternatively, you might find yourself at your deadline eating breakfast in bed that has been brought to you by a new, more loving partner, so be very careful how you word your goals and the way you direct your mind.

Destiny

You have no control over other people, places or things, you know that, however, you are the master of your own destiny.

There is a frequently used AA saying, 'Let go and let God.' If you believe in a higher power, this is a very good statement to live by. In essence it says that once you've done your best, you need to let God or the Universe do the rest.

You do not have the power to ruin God's or the Universe's plans but you do have the power to make the most of the life you have been blessed with.

Have courage for the great sorrows of life and patience for the small ones; and when you have laboriously accomplished your daily task, go to sleep in peace. God is awake: Victor Hugo.

Detach But Still Love

In many ways you are powerless to make your loved one stop drinking. The first crucial step in being able to detach yourself from the situation is by realising that the actions of the alcoholic are not your problem or your responsibility. If you have completed the exercises in the book thus far, I'm sure you are well on your way to fully understanding this and are changing your way of thinking.

You have the power to be the owner of your actions and to allow your alcoholic partner and other family members to own theirs, gradually, or suddenly in some cases. This could make them finally realise that they have a problem as they look at the destructive consequences of their actions. Your ability to change the way you deal with things is well within your power.

You can listen to and identify with other peoples' pain or joy without having to own it or trying to control it. By learning to take care of your own life and allowing others including your alcoholic partner to tend to theirs, you can detach without losing compassion.

Don't Play Games

We all want instant sobriety; it can only come with time. Sometimes it's tempting to set up situations that embarrass them into becoming sober or makes things more awkward for them. Don't do this, it only takes up valuable head space and makes you a person you don't want to be.

Remember, from this point on recovery is about you, not the alcoholic. By looking after yourself and no longer taking responsibility for the actions of another adult, you will soon learn how to have the freedom to be yourself again and still love and care about the feelings of others, without having to be in control of them.

Chapter 14

What Is Normality?

I realise life is precious, amusing, eventful and full of opportunity and no matter what you believe happens to us when we die, it's clear we only have one shot at this life.

To fully realise this, you don't have to put flowers in your hair or dance around naked under a full moon, nor do you have to pledge to be constantly happy no matter how other people affect you. On the contrary, you should allow yourself to feel angry towards them if you wish, but still love them.

You can get through the hurt they have caused you without giving up on love. You can experience deep sadness but recognise and know that life does not always have to be like a roller-coaster ride and those high points don't have to be followed by plummeting dips.

Feelings

When you live with an alcohol dependent, you can become somewhat reluctant to show your true feelings. However, when you're happy, give in to it, don't pre-empt the possible low that may or may not follow, concentrate on enjoying your joyful moment.

One of my most memorable nights at after-care came when another wife and I realised that being happy without conditional lows, was what living normally was all about. We realised there didn't have to be a great big dip with a devastating, heart-wrenching low afterwards if we allowed ourselves to feel happy. We started to laugh with joy at this realisation and couldn't stop. We couldn't believe how great it felt to live normally.

Many people take this for granted but those who live with an alcoholic find it very hard to do. Our emotions become bland and we become cynical.

I used to cry whilst watching sad movies but during my time living with an active alcoholic, I found I'd just criticise and make fun of the scenes that would have pulled at my heart strings previously.

I'd stopped fully experiencing my range of emotions and once I dropped the barrier that protected me, I gradually allowed myself to enjoy films again like I used to.

Now I cry at every family occasion, every daft movie or television show that provokes emotions of absolute happiness or deep sadness and confess that those big reveals they do on DIY shows get me every time!

Exercise 8: Dreams

In your notebook, make a list of the dreams you want to fulfil and the activities you enjoy which your partner's alcoholism is preventing you from doing. There are no rules here, they can be as outrageous as you like.

Begin each sentence with, 'If it were not for my partner's addiction I would...'

My list included travel the world or at least go on holiday twice a year, have some savings, start my own company and be my own boss, spend more time enjoying my children, socialise more, not cry from sadness every day but with laughter instead and be less worried and anxious.

Up to that point in time, I wasn't taking action to follow the life I wanted to live, I was living in reaction to my loved one's destructive actions through drinking; I was following his lead.

There was only one possible outcome for me. My life inevitably stagnated and my partner's drinking dictated how I would spend my days emotionally and physically.

He didn't intend for this to happen, he was too caught up in his own life which revolved around alcohol and I was interfering with how he chose to live.

When you're living with an alcoholic, their actions are bound to cross over the threads of your life. What you need to do is regain control and become a leader of your own path, not a follower of theirs. You have to stop living with someone else's lifestyle choices, stop existing to fulfil their needs and stop settling for less than what you want from your life.

As soon as I realised I wasn't a victim who allowed my loved one's actions and behaviour to control my every waking moment, I realised I could do everything on my list and right now, the only person stopping you from doing all the things on your list, is you, not the alcoholic.

By trying to control their actions and predict their behaviour, you're filling up lots of important head space which could be used to realise your dreams.

Remember, you cannot change or control other people but you can change and control your own actions, reactions and thoughts.

Trust that making positive changes to your situation will bring about the best results, accept the fact that there might be discomfort during the transition and you may encounter unlikely or unwanted outcomes but know ultimately that you will triumph!

Respect

People who live with an alcoholic sometimes confuse compassion with love and this can make them stay with their partner because it's easier.

A vital element in a successful and happy relationship is respect and you should not only love your partner but respect them too and be proud of who they are. Equally, your partner should have the same feelings towards you but this is probably not the case at the moment, however it is something to strive towards.

Exercise 9: To Do List

Use your notebook to create a to do list for anything you want to get done. If you want to lose a bit of weight, schedule in a little exercise time or make a date to go swimming or out for a run.

You can also find new recipes and plan to change your diet by including healthier food options and cutting out a few takeaways.

If your goal is to have a better relationship with your children, write different suggestions for ways you can spend time with them each day, maybe getting them to help you cook dinner or simply bake a cake.

You could also assist them with homework, read them a bedtime story or replace television time with a hot chocolate and some conversation.

Fluid discussions about all sorts of topics will blossom in due course once you clear your deck and dedicate time to your children.

Don't let their lives pass you by, take action but understand that changes can be difficult to effect initially and you have to apply yourself to them fully to make them work.

At the end of each day, list five things in your notebook or head that you've accomplished and go to sleep thinking about the things you are thankful for.

When you concentrate on your progress, the challenges you have no control over will begin to look after themselves. By making a positive change within, you'll create a force which will help everyone around you.

You have found your way to reading this book because you're living with an alcohol dependent partner and you can find a better way of living your life; it's a real positive in a negative situation and you are about to change everything.

Chapter 15

To Stay Or To Go

Families with alcohol related problems live in painful chaos. It's disturbing and hurtful to watch the one you love change like this. It horrible being lied to, feeling insecure, ashamed and constantly disappointed.

The partner of an alcoholic slides into a tough existence often filled with mutual accusations and obsession with experiments to control the alcoholic and can easily forget about their own and their children's needs.

The road to freedom begins with the understanding that you are powerless when it comes to their drinking, that you only can take responsibility for your own life and that you can and must refuse to suffer alongside the alcoholic when they drink.

It is OK to decide that you do not want to live with your alcoholic partner any more. This is not a sign that you have failed in your relationship or in your duties to them as a partner.

Think back to when you knew this person before their excessive drinking took hold of them. Perhaps you've never known them without alcohol, in which case you need to think back to a period of sobriety in their lives that you have experienced. Ask yourself honestly, did you like that person and what was it about them you loved?

Exercise 10: Relief, Stability And Growth

Use a piece of paper for this exercise, not your notebook.

Write out the following question and list your answers:

If (their name) was sober, how could he/she contribute towards making my life better?

Make a list as long as you like and remember, no one else is going to see it. You are going to burn it afterwards so be completely honest with yourself.

Split the list into three categories; relief, stability and growth. Here are a few examples that might help:

Relief:

- I wouldn't feel quite so anxious all the time
- I wouldn't live in fear of what was going to happen
- We wouldn't argue as much
- The children would bring their friends home again

Stability:

- If they got a job they could contribute to the bills
- They could help with the household chores again
- We could sit and have family meals together
- They could actively contribute to family life
- They could assist the children with homework
- They could spend time playing with children
- We could live within our budget

Growth:

- I could share my problems and feel supported
- They could encourage me to achieve my dreams
- They would be my friend again and support me on a day-to-day basis
- Our sex life would be better
- We could have friends over again
- We would laugh again like we used to
- We could make plans for our old age

Note how the word *again* has come up several times in the sample list. This is because if alcohol was no longer part of your loved one's life they would probably revert back to being a similar person to the one they were before alcohol addiction. Bear in mind, however, they are unlikely to transform into something they never were.

Sometimes people describe recovered addicts as being either very boring or very serious. This is generally because they've been more commonly recognised as being the rowdy one and over the top for quite some time.

The question you need to ask yourself in due course is, if they become sober, will you still want to live with them?

If you can't establish how you feel about this, why are you trying to encourage them to be sober? Do you feel guilt? Do you feel it is your duty to stand by them?

Of course, if it is your parent, child or another blood relative who is drinking heavily, presumably you'd want to help them to become sober because they are family.

By re-familiarising yourself with the qualities your partner has and their overall appeal when they do not drink, it will help steer you towards your goal and aid your transformation into a stronger, better person. It is also hoped your partner will want to achieve the same result for themselves.

When Children Are Involved

Children living with an alcoholic parent frequently try to be perfect so as not to feel they are causing them to drink, or they misbehave to get attention because the drinker takes centre-stage. They misguidedly think that if they were a better child, the alcoholic would stop drinking, not realising that the drinking has nothing whatsoever to do with the child's behaviour.

Children of alcoholics run the risk of becoming as sick as the alcoholic themselves. They regularly take on responsibilities they are not ready for because the alcoholic is not being responsible. They often assume the role of the missing alcoholic parent by preparing meals, cleaning the house, taking care of other siblings, working after school to help pay bills and undertaking many other duties that the alcoholic parent has shirked.

If you have allowed your children to suffer the effects of your partner's alcoholism, then you'll have to make amends. This won't be a simple matter of saying you're sorry either. I recognise this is probably one of the hardest things you'll have to face up to and deal with, but remember, you are in the process of gaining a new understanding of your world and must promise yourself that you'll never allow the same thing to happen again.

If It Wasn't For The Children
I Would Leave

If you've ever uttered these words, I want you to answer the following questions in your notebook:

1. How miserable is your life at the moment on a scale of one to ten, with ten being the worst?

2. Has your alcoholic loved one ever hit or hurt your children, or threatened them so much that it frightened them and/or you?

3. Has your alcoholic loved one ever hit you in front of, or within earshot of your children?

4. Does your alcoholic loved one drive the car with your children in it after they have been drinking?

5. Has your alcoholic partner ever been rendered unconscious from drink while looking after the children alone?

6. Does your alcoholic loved one have loud arguments, shout insults at you, or break things during drink-fuelled disagreements in front of the children?

If you answered yes to one or more of the questions, your excuse of staying because of the children holds no water.

By staying, you are endangering your children's mental and physical health. You also need to affirm to the children that this behaviour is entirely unacceptable in any loving relationship.

Many partners of alcoholics see themselves as victims, innocent victims of the other person's abuse, but you have to take responsibility now and change that pattern.

If your partner has harmed your child emotionally or physically on more than one occasion while you have lived with them, you have harmed them too.

By allowing the same pattern to continue and by not changing your ways, you have allowed this circle of abuse to remain unbroken. If your children are in harm's way, you need to move them out of the situation, immediately.

They Are A Great Parent
When They're Not Drinking

The alcoholic in your life may be the best parent in the world without drink and that's probably why you're reading this book, because you want to stay with them.

They are aware of their shortcomings and will often overcompensate by buying the children gifts or being over the top with outings or affection when they're sober. Of course, no child can ever have too much affection but a parents' affection should be constant and not arrive in bouts. This type of volatile behaviour can be incredibly confusing for a child.

Your child may appear to prefer your spouse over you at times and you might feel as though the youngster is never as expressive of their affections with you, leaving you feeling resentful, jealous or depressed about this.

Children are very clever, so when a drinking parent shows them inconsistent levels of love they will often go overboard in demonstrating their love and affection when their parent is in a positive, playful mood. That's because they want to please them. It's their way of illustrating their approval of the good behaviour of the parent. What they're trying to convey is, 'This is how it can always be, look how much I can love you and if you behave like this all the time, I will love you more than anybody else in the world.'

When your partner drinks again and behaves badly, the child may regress in a variety of ways, becoming hard or cross with you. If they present as angry towards you it's invariably because they are confused. They are subconsciously blaming you for the alcoholic's drinking and might also simply need to take their heartbreak out on somebody close to home. Trying to deal with this and cope with your alcoholic partner just makes life seem so unfair, doesn't it?

Think about your impenetrable wall, the barrier you put up to deflect the hurt that descends when your partner lets you down, well children develop barriers too. Your children probably have one in place and if you don't do something about the situation, their wall is only going to get stronger and harder for them to break down and this is very likely to affect their own relationships in adulthood.

Research collated by the National Association for Children of Alcoholics in the UK (NACOA) shows that over one third of children who experience problems with alcoholic parents carry them into their adult life. Parental alcohol abuse has also been shown to be a risk factor for premature death, suicide attempts, mental illness, drug addiction and teenage motherhood.

In the UK, NACOA offer a free helpline and have extensive resources available to children of alcohol dependent parents (that's youngsters and adult children too, incidentally) and they receive over 600 requests for help every month. There are also other international branches of NACOA with similar services, see the Resources pages at the back of the book for details.

The mental guard that you've created to make your life more functional with your alcoholic loved one is not easily dropped which means your children are not experiencing you as the best parent you could be.

Your partner may be receiving demonstrations of love from your children when they're sober and you might be receiving indifferent behaviour from the children, as you lack the time and emotional capability to show them all the love you want to.

Signs Of Distress In Children

I recall an acquaintance who was living in an alcohol dependent relationship telling me that their children didn't know anything about it. She claimed they never argued in front of the children and that she ensured they didn't witness any of the negative effects of their father's drinking. Children are incredibly proficient actors and they're not stupid. If there is a long-term problem in your house, they'll know something isn't right, however, they might also think the volatile behaviour they experience is the norm and until they compare that to normal behaviour in other people's houses, they may not see it as being something that is wrong.

Does your child do any of the following?

- Wet the bed
- Withdraw from daily life
- Rock when relaxing
- Display clingy behaviour
- Comfort eat or show a loss of appetite
- Have nightmares

These are a tiny handful of the signs children present with when they are emotionally distressed.

Your children may become upset from the changes you are about to make, but at the moment they are probably experiencing a family atmosphere of hostility and lies rather than love and cooperation. It's your responsibility to upset the balance in order to achieve a healthier, happier and safer family environment for them and you.

The children depend on your leadership so look ahead and act now to secure the kind of family you want to have in the future. It may well be a hard road but you can learn a great deal from everything that unfolds and grow stronger than you ever imagined in the process.

Physical Abuse

Never, under any circumstances, accept physical abuse towards you or your children. All alcoholics are emotionally abusive to those they live with, selfishness is a statutory part of their disease and they'll do whatever it takes to justify their drinking or relieve their guilt.

That said, not all alcoholics are physically violent. If you are experiencing any level of physical abuse, do not under any circumstances, put up with it.

Your life and the lives of other members of your family are far more important than living in fear or danger.

Emotional abuse can be healed once a situation is brought under control but physical abuse can leave lasting scars both physical and emotional, which may never heal.

Your partner may threaten to keep hold of the children if you leave the family home and/or threaten to kill you, the children or themselves if you leave.

This threat should be taken very seriously as you are clearly living a life of fear, not a life of choice. We only have one shot at life and one chance of giving our children a safe childhood.

As long as you continue to respond to your partner's threats, you are putting yourself and your children in a vulnerable position and in the direct line of fire for their destructive behaviour and escalating intimidation.

You do not need to ask your partner for permission to leave them or for a separation, you simply need to leave with your children. You are an adult with more rights than you realise and your partner is not in charge of custody decisions, this will be made with a great deal of support from other services that keep the children's safety and best interests at their core.

If violence has been an issue in your relationship, you need to take the lead right now and find out exactly what your rights are in a calm and secure environment, like the house of a trusted friend or family member, or from a refuge. In the UK there are refuges for women, refuges for men and some specifically for members of the LGBT community, many of which will allow your children to be with you. There are undoubtedly similar resources available in other countries too.

This step is enormous and I realise it can be an incredibly difficult one to take, particularly as your self-confidence may have been shattered over the years of living under your partner's control. However, there are a great many agencies and support groups that offer free legal and professional aid to help you understand your entitlements. Once armed with this knowledge, you can develop a course of action that will ensure the safety of you and your children; see the Resources pages for details.

Avoiding Confrontation

Arguments, tension and confrontation are common daily occurrences when living with an alcoholic. Avoidance of interaction with the alcoholic while they are drinking is the best solution and this includes, talking and arguing with them.

They aren't able to think clearly when they are drunk and won't take in what you say, so why waste your breath arguing about their behaviour? Why fuss and fight with someone who has lost the ability to make sense? Don't become ensnared in the alcoholic trap with them, instead stay out of the trap, work your way through this book and you will soon be able to help them.

Alcoholics are frequently confrontational, so it is better to avoid them when they are getting drunk. This is, of course, far easier said than done.

You could try going to bed early or setting up your own area of relaxation in the house. If they follow you and try to draw you into an argument, ask if you can talk about it in the morning instead.

However tempting it may be, don't say, 'You're drunk, I'm not discussing it with you', as this will only add fuel to the fire. Instead reply with something like, 'I'm feeling too tired to discuss this at the moment, can we talk about it tomorrow?'

Your partner may well continue to rant and rave but stick firmly to your calm lines and hopefully they will leave you alone.

When they're sober, address the issue and tell them you're ready to talk about their issues of the night before. There's a high likelihood they won't be able to remember having the conversation or the context of it and will try to brush it off.

Take this opportunity to drop a few reminders of the hurtful things that were said, however, don't gloat, nag or labour the point.

If you don't feel comfortable doing this, don't do it. This isn't about winning a mind game but hopefully it'll be enough to remind them of their behaviour and gradually over time, they'll realise they are having blackouts and being nasty.

Confronting The Alcoholic In Your Life

When confronting your partner about their drinking, be sure to do it in a loving way. Don't yell, accuse or threaten them, instead tell them you're concerned about their drinking and express your concern that they may have a serious problem.

Following a calm discussion, they may try to reduce it but if you are still bothered by their habit and behaviour, it's important that you do something to help yourself.

Do not enable them to drink or become obsessed with their alcohol consumption. More often than not the alcoholic doesn't actually want any help but it's important that you seek help for yourself and the rest of the family.

When the time is right, make it clear that you are always there to talk about their problems and are willing to help and support them to find a solution. In that conversation, you will have to try to motivate the drinker to change their view of the situation.

Here are a few important points related to this:

1. Make the drinker feel positive about themselves. Many drinkers have self-loathing and peg themselves as useless. Don't reproach, instead pay them compliments about the things they do that go right and reinforce it with the reasons why you love and want to support them.

2. Take away the prejudices about treatment such as the idea that people are always hospitalised, that therapy only consists of talking, or that others will judge them.

3. Give your partner a new perspective. Positive examples you can use are they'll have more money if they don't drink, they'll have better contact with their family, better health too and improved prospects for work.

4. Listen to potential problems they flag up that might make them keep drinking but indicate that alcohol won't solve them, it will only make them worse.

5. If they don't want to receive help, or feel they cannot be helped, ask what needs to happen to convince them they need to get treatment.

Be ready to assist on every level and begin by collating all the information you can on various methods of treatment. If they agree to accept treatment, you will have done the research and be ready to discuss all the options with them.

When They Admit They Need Help

When your partner hits rock bottom and if they finally admit they need help, don't jump up yelling, 'Yippee, I told you so!'

Admitting they have a problem is the first big step but be prepared for them to take one step forward and ten steps back.

Don't get too excited or smug, instead stay calm and relaxed and encourage them to see a professional to discuss what's available to help them decide how they want to proceed.

Show them the research you did and suggest they begin with an appointment with their GP, or if they really want to steam ahead, discuss a rehab centre that might be able to assist and offer to get the ball rolling.

Whilst it is important to be ready and willing to help, it's equally important that you don't take the responsibility upon yourself, without your partner having asked for it, otherwise everything will go the same way.

The alcohol dependent needs to understand that their recovery depends on them wanting it and them making it happen and that you are there to support their decision and positive actions.

Offer to accompany them on their visit to the GP, or to call rehab centres to seek a place, or to make an appointment for them to see a counsellor. It is helpful if you're involved in the initial discussions with your GP or counsellor, as an alcoholic often hears what they want to hear and frequently come back with a misconstrued version of the advice or diagnosis. I do know a person who was convinced their doctor said, 'Yes, you are an alcoholic but you can have a few pints in the pub.'

My husband believed the doctor told him he had Hepatitis B and only had six months to live but it was nothing to do with alcohol. When I heard that I was devastated, in complete shock and utterly gob-smacked. Then I thought about it for a while, there had been no blood tests, no consulting with me, his wife. I telephoned the doctor and he didn't have Hepatitis B, but the doctor had warned him that he was going to have liver failure if he continued.

All subsequent dramatic health results he came back with were taken with a pinch of salt.

So, if your partner allows you, do accompany them or at least offer to drive them to appointments, but if they insist on going alone, let them. After all, this is their responsibility and you are only there in a support capacity.

Even once the appointments have been made, they may back out because they feel they're not ready to give up alcohol or the thought of a detox is too severe.

One of the scariest thoughts for an alcoholic to contemplate is the idea of never having another drink, ever again. A good point my husband learned from and lived by after rehab was, yes he could drink again and that it was up to him to decide if he wanted to or not.

This concept is very empowering for them, as there is no one other than the alcoholic saying whether they are allowed to drink or not; it is entirely up to them to decide if drink is that important.

Chapter 16

Sobriety

Living with a recovering alcoholic isn't easy but it is possible with a great deal of effort from both partners. If you both invest that time and you eventually find yourself with a sober partner, that is wonderful, however, it's also important to realise sobriety brings its own challenges.

I don't want to burst your bubble, but if your partner attains sobriety, it doesn't necessarily mean you'll live happily ever after. All marriages and partnerships require positive effort and the absence of alcohol and the chaos that goes with it can also bring about drastic changes in their personality.

Think about this scenario for a moment; they were the person who was always the centre of the party and they now prefer to decline parties and social events. They sleep more, spend more time alone reading, or are always out at Alcoholics Anonymous meetings which you can't go to.

They're trying to take on responsibilities that you feel are your territory and you find it hard to let go. They aren't talking to you as much and you may even miss the drama of those old arguments you used to have!

Sex, communication and responsibilities can all change and worse still, some of the problems you used to be able to put down to drink, are still there. It turns out it's just their personality! How tough is that?

After all that effort, they might decide to continue to spend money foolishly, they still talk out of line to you and they still don't want to play with the kids.

Sobriety can also bring a know-it-all attitude where they start articulating all of your faults which led to them starting to drink and advise you that it's you that needs to change.

If you still enjoy a drink, they might start pointing their finger saying you need to be aware of over-indulging! You might think to yourself, how dare they tell you you're at fault, after all you've been through!

Your partner may have been through an intensive rehab programme learning techniques to get their life back on track and stay sober and sometimes we feel like we're at a loose end. After taking care of everything for so long, it can be hard to stop trying to control everything and to let go of looking after the other person.

When our partners become sober, it's more important than ever to start looking after ourselves. It is OK to feel angry, confused or disappointment along with the joy and excitement about the new situation.

Whether your partner is drinking or sober, it's important to accept that couples have disagreements without either one being solely to blame. You don't have to place the blame or keep score of how well you've performed in the defence position. Instead of pointing the finger and wasting hours of your life mulling it over, assess your part in the conflict and try to ensure it doesn't happen again.

Alcoholism is a disease and just like any other serious illness it has a list of associated symptoms. Whilst living with an active alcoholic, one often encounters additional complexities such as anxiety, anger, denial, obsession, control, guilt and self-doubt thrown into the mix to fix.

These destructive elements are not only projected onto the alcohol dependent and their partner, but onwards and outwards to other relationships too. By recognising them and accepting that you too need to change and heal, you will start your journey on the road to reclaiming your self-esteem, self-worth and love of life.

Chapter 17

Summary
And A Final Warning

From this point onwards, your identity is no longer that of a wife, husband, lover or partner of an alcoholic and the only person responsible for your quality of life, is you.

Furthermore, you must accept that your partner is the only person who can stop themselves drinking and make their life worth living.

You are an individual, with amazing potential and entirely responsible for your actions, your words, your emotions and your decisions. You didn't cause the situation you are in, you can't control it and you cannot cure it either.

Take Care Of Yourself

Go to the Al-Anon meetings you wrote about in your notebook as many times a week as you need to. It's a vital and completely anonymous service and will be an extremely supportive and helpful part of your healing and recovery.

Cast your mind back to what I said at the beginning of this book; think hard about the emergency instructions they give you at the start of a flight and attend to your own mask, then help those around you. Get yourself on an even keel first and then you'll be in the best position to help the ones you love.

Live by the following advice on a daily basis; free yourself from resentment, bitterness and anger, try to please yourself first, keep an open mind, make healthy lifestyle choices, stop being concerned about what other people might think, express your ideas and feelings, learn that it is OK to say, 'No'.

Stick to your values and make yourself the best person you can possibly be.

If you follow these guidelines you will have done the best you can to empower yourself with a renewed strength and willpower to help others.

Alcohol dependants sometimes find sobriety after their partner has been going to Al-Anon for a while. As their partner gets better and grows in strength, the situation improves. By you continuing to be a positive example, the alcoholic is stripped of their denial and can open themselves up to seek sobriety. Don't bet on it, but don't discount it either.

Remove the victim from volatile situations; don't stand there and take it, know you have the ability to walk away, go for a drive, or run an errand.

Most importantly, don't try to reason with someone who is inebriated. By definition, a person who is intoxicated is incapable of any sane reasoning or judgement.

Don't put away your partner's empty bottles any more, stop buying their drink and quit cleaning up their mess. In order for your partner to turn their life around, they have to stop liking the way they're living.

There is no need to exaggerate anything any more and don't encourage or stage bad things to happen. Let your partner live with the full consequences of their actions so they can completely understand what's happening and realise precisely what they're doing. Do not create crisis or prevent crisis either.

You've read the book, you've poured your heart out in your private notebook and you now understand that alcohol was affecting your partner and you too! Now it's time to tend to and repair your own mental and physical health and take courage to develop your recovery plan.

Whatever plans you make, this must be my parting advice; if you are experiencing any form of domestic violence, put the children and pets in the car and leave.

Violence almost always escalates, it rarely subsides and once you're on the roller-coaster of physical abuse, it's very tough to get off. Battered wife or husband syndrome is frighteningly common and can leave its victims feeling as though they're trapped under the most powerfully hypnotic evil spell.

They start to believe there's nothing out there for them and that they're undesirable, unworthy and completely deserving of the abuse. If you're trapped in that lonely place, getting out will be very difficult but you absolutely must trust and heed my advice and get out immediately.

Divorce might be something you want to consider but put that thought aside for a moment and focus on what you need to do. There are lots of support groups available and they will be able to point you in the right direction, but for now, stop being a victim of physical abuse and don't walk, run!

I sincerely hope the situation with your alcohol dependent partner hasn't descended to this and hope you have a clearer vision of what you need to do next. I also trust you've found comfort, strength, guidance and a renewed sense of self from reading this book.

Remember, both happiness and change come from within and you can learn and grow from everything you experience in this life.

For further advice, resources and for ongoing support from me, please visit **HowToLiveWithAnAlcoholic.com**.

This is your life, make it a good one!

Afterword

By Rob B Windsor

There's nothing more sobering than hearing a personal life experience of someone connected to an individual in addiction, with its heartbreak and the destruction of a family unit often being one of the complications of this disease. Sadly, my experience of caring for anyone with an addiction doesn't begin to touch the surface of the struggles that their partners, children and families have had to endure.

I work as a Registered General Nurse at Clouds House, a residential treatment centre run by the charity Action on Addiction. As a result of my work, I have met several hundred alcohol dependents. This by no means makes me an expert, however, it does make me a credible witness. A witness to the lives of countless addicts and families who have been troubled by this terrible illness.

I look at the process of recovering from alcohol addiction using a medical analogy; you observe a simple cut or graze becoming inflamed, painful and uncomfortable, before it finally settles down and repairs. Like a deep wound, emotional healing for all parties has to begin from within. Scars invariably remain but they are reduced considerably if the process is careful, open and honest.

We ask our clients to focus initially on repairing themselves. You can't look at the wider picture unless you start on the central problem. Thoughts of building a house on sand come to mind.

It's a selfish disease, not a choice or way of life. It's an illness that affects the whole family and untreated, it can end in the death of an individual and the death of a family.

I recognise many of the issues raised by Lilly's honest and proactive book including the, 'Yes but' retort and concur that all too often, we give solutions or guide the alcoholic to seek their own solution, only to receive the, 'Yes but' repost. I've often found myself having to step back, raise an eyebrow and say, 'For every solution, you present another problem. You now need to stop hoarding the problems, empty your shelves and fix the brackets!' This self-help book packed with first-hand experience is one you should put on your revamped shelves.

Yes but there are too many self-help books to chose from with too much information...

This book is different. It is easy to follow, it speaks from experience, it's not preachy or prescriptive. It comes from the soul of a lady who has lived through close attachment to an addict, who has experienced the excuses, the empty promises and the let downs. She has also come up and out the other side with her recovered alcoholic husband; her process worked.

Lilly's book is a perfect accompaniment and resource for anyone struggling in isolation.

Rob B Windsor
RN, DipPHC(DN)
BSc(Hons) Clinical Leadership

Biography

As well as working at Clouds House, since 2011 Rob has also built up a portfolio of work as a creative director with his company, Facing Tides Theatre in Education. It includes a linked trilogy of powerful dramas that focus on various types of addiction and alcoholism runs through them all.

They were written and are directed by Rob and have been staged in theatres and educational establishments alike, along with post-performance outreach workshops. These exploratory dramas seek to empower individuals to find solutions to help themselves or discover how to find the help they or a family member may need.

For further details see
FacingTidesTheatre.co.uk

Resources

Action on Addiction
A registered charity that offers treatment centres throughout England including a specialist family service, innovative research programmes and an expert training centre
www.actiononaddiction.org.uk
General enquiries 0300 330 0659

Addaction
They aim to help transform the lives of people affected by drug and alcohol problems by offering a wide range of services in England and Scotland
www.addaction.org.uk

Adfam
A national charity working with families affected by drugs and alcohol. Adfam operates an online message board and database of local support groups
www.adfam.org.uk
General enquiries 0207 553 7640

Adult Children of Alcoholics
A recovery programme for children whose lives were affected as a result of being raised with an alcoholic or dysfunctional family. It is based on the success of the Twelve Steps of Alcoholics Anonymous and employs its version of the Twelve Steps and Twelve Traditions
www.adultchildren.org

Al-Anon

Provides support to anyone whose life is, or has been, affected by someone else's drinking, regardless of whether that person is still drinking or not

www.al-anonuk.org.uk

Helpline 0207 403 0888

www.al-anon.org for various international sites

Alateen

Provides support for teenage relatives and friends of alcoholics and is part of Al-Anon. Their meetings can be attended by 12-17 year olds who meet to share experiences caused by the problem drinker in their lives

www.al-anonuk.org.uk/alateen

For meetings 0207 407 0215

www.al-anon.alateen.org for various international sites

Alcoholics Anonymous Great Britain

A fellowship of men and women who share their experience, strength and hope with each other in order to solve their common problems and help others to recover from alcoholism

www.alcoholics-anonymous.org.uk

Helpline 0845 769 7555

Alcohol Concern

Our goal is to improve people's lives through reducing the harm caused by alcohol. We have an ambitious long-term aim to change the drinking culture in this country.

www.alcoholconcern.org.uk

General enquiries 0207 566 9800

Aiséirí Treatment Centres
Offer addiction treatment centres in Cahir Co Tipperary, Roxborough Wexford and Ballybeg Waterford in Ireland
www.aiseiri.ie

Broken Rainbow
The first and only UK organisation dedicated to confronting and eliminating domestic violence within and against the LGBT communities. Refuge information also available
www.brokenrainbow.org.uk
0300 999 5428

Carers Direct
Information, advice and support from the NHS for all carers covering a wide range of topics including financial and legal issues, through to respite care and access to local services
www.nhs.uk/carersdirect
Helpline 0300 123 1053

Children of Addicted Parents and People
COAP was founded by Emma Spiegler to help establish connections between young people affected by parental and family drug and alcohol abuse and other addictions such as gambling via online counselling and message boards
www.coap.org.uk
Admin only 0207 763 6270

Clouds House Residential Treatment Centre
Offer a well-structured treatment programme for you to learn about yourself in relation to addiction, your vulnerability to relapse and how you can sustain recovery by working with the 12-step abstinence based philosophy. Family treatment also available
www.actiononaddiction.org.uk/treatment/clouds-house.aspx
Admissions 01747 832 070

Drink Aware
Promotes responsible drinking and finds innovative ways to challenge the national drinking culture to help reduce alcohol misuse and minimise alcohol-related harm
www.drinkaware.co.uk

Drinkline
If you're worried about your own or someone else's drinking, you can call this free helpline, in complete confidence
Helpline 0300 123 1110

Get A Divorce
Everything you need to know about the legal grounds for and filing for divorce including all the necessary papers in the UK. Many of these can be completed online or printed out
www.gov.uk/divorce

Mankind Initiative

Support for male victims of domestic abuse and domestic violence and vital links to refuges that can take you and your children if you are in danger
www.mankind.org.uk
National Helpline 01823 334 244

National Association for Children of Alcoholics

NACOA offer an invaluable confidential, free helpline and comprehensive website that addresses the needs of children growing up in families where one or both parents suffer from alcoholism or a similar addictive problem. They help young and adult children of alcoholics
www.nacoa.org.uk
Helpline 0800 358 3456

The Princess Royal Trust for Carers

Through a network of 144 carers centres and websites, the trust provides information, advice and support services to 368,000 carers, including 20,000 young carers, including those who are affected by looking after alcohol addicted parents
www.youngcarers.net
www.carers.org
General enquiries 0844 800 4361

Rehab Online

A directory of residential rehabilitation and detox services and centres for adult drug and/or alcohol addicts in England and Wales
www.rehab-online.org.uk

Saint John of God Hospital

Since 1882 the mission of Saint John of God Hospital in Stillorgan, Co Dublin has been to bring healing, care and wholeness to people who have mental illness or psychological and emotional problems including alcohol addiction

www.stjohnofgodhospital.ie

+353 1 277 1400

Samaritans

A 24 hour, 365 days of the year helpline service for anyone struggling with tough times, particularly if they are feeling suicidal. They can help you explore your options, understand your problems better, or simply be there to listen

www.samaritans.org

Helpline UK 08457 90 90 90

Helpline ROI +353 1 850 60 90 90

Stepchat

Online chat rooms who welcome everyone whose life has been affected by alcoholism and substance abuse with virtual discussion rooms available 24 hours a day with no country barriers

www.stepchat.com

Womens Aid

A national charity working to end domestic violence against women and children with a network of over 300 dedicated specialist services across the UK

www.womensaid.org.uk

Free 24 Hour Helpline 0808 2000 247

Your Notes

Lightning Source UK Ltd.
Milton Keynes UK
UKOW05f1932210214

226939UK00006B/74/P

9 781910 094068